R D B

RICHMOND

NOV 1995

Charters
on
Charting

First published 1995

© David Charters

British Library Cataloguing in Publication Data. A catalogue record for this book is available from the British Library.

ISBN 0 948035 21 8

Published by:
Rushmere Wynne Ltd.
Cavalier House, 21 High Street,
Leighton Buzzard,
Bedfordshire LU7 7DN.

Printed by:
H S Printers Ltd.
Buzzard Works,
Billington Road,
Leighton Buzzard,
Bedfordshire, LU7 8IN.

CHARTERS
ON
CHARTING

by

David Charters

Rushmere Wynne
England

*To my parents who sacrificed so much for me,
my wife, Kath, who has tolerated hours of loneliness while
this book was written, and to my colleagues
at Investment Research of Cambridge,
without whose enthusiasm and dedication
my professional career could not have developed.*

*My special thanks are also due to Jon Foster whose illustrations
have brought this book alive.*

✼

CONTENTS

Although every attempt has been made to explain the terminology of Charting, the vocabulary of stockmarket investment is extensive. A complete introduction to the subject, and the language used, can be found in *The Investors' Handbook* by Maggie Drummond and introduced by Sir John Harvey-Jones. The ISBN is 0-948035-04-8. It is available from most business bookshops, some branches of W. H. Smith or direct from the publishers, Rushmere Wynne Limited.

The special offer referred to on the cover of this book can be found on pages 90 - 91.

INTRODUCTION

"Stocks and shares go up and down,
but not necessarily in that order"– **Anon.**

Anyone involved in investing in securities markets has learned how difficult it is to anticipate how prices are going to move. And the occasions when it becomes most difficult to do so are often those where the biggest profits can be lost or opportunities missed. When bull markets turn into bear markets and vice-versa, when the economic or political news is all good, or bad, these are the times when your profits could be maximised.

One way to tackle the problem is to maintain and analyse charts, or graphs, of price movements. Stories exist from centuries ago in the rice markets of the Far East of dealers and traders keeping records of day-to-day price movements in order to establish when trends occurred in prices. By plotting these price changes on graph paper it was noticed that certain patterns repeated themselves time and again. And trends of price movements were observed to persist, sometimes for quite long periods of time.

This was the beginning of Charting, or, as it is known in professional circles, Technical Analysis. For the purposes of this book we will stick with the name "Charting".

I have used price charts for a quarter of a century and my company has used them since 1945. There is no doubt at all in my mind that to use and interpret them to analyse the behaviour of the prices themselves is invaluable. And when used in conjunction with more widely accepted forms of analysis the investor will have more power to his or her strategy and tactics than most of the other participators in the market.

Many textbooks have been written about charting. Most go very deeply into the subject and some are highly mathematical. This book has been written with the beginner in mind and should be a first step in a very important direction. By the time you have digested the contents you should begin to make better – and more timely – decisions. I hope you will become encouraged to read further. Whether you are relatively experienced as an investor, or are just beginning to get to grips with the market, there are lessons here for you to learn.

David Charters,
Cambridge
March 1995

ONE

WHAT IS CHARTING?

Do you ever get the feeling that prices go their own way, on a seemingly erratic course which bears little resemblance to what is happening to the economy as a whole, or to the company in which you have invested?

The simple reason is that stocks and shares go up and down because people buy and sell them. They are subject to the very same laws of supply and demand as most other goods. When, for example, there is a shortage of coffee the price rises to choke off demand so why shouldn't shares be the same? After all there are a limited number of them issued by any one company. If too many investors are chasing after them the price will go up until some holders of the shares are persuaded to sell; this, in turn, meets the demand.

For example, at the beginning of 1994 the share price of British Telecom, the largest of the privatisation issues, stood at 490p and yet just four months later they had fallen to 360p – just over 25% lower. BT was the same company with the same products but investors must have felt that the price was too high at 490p and held off until it was low enough to tempt them again. The share price then bounced sharply as buyers re-entered the market and the price crossed the 400p level again, if only temporarily.

Too often investors commit the fatal error of confusing a company with its shares. The company's profits and general trading outlook have a large bearing on the share price but it is foolish to believe, as many do, that they are the be-all-and-end-all of the argument. Many factors influence the price of the shares.

Share prices are determined by dozens of elements, only one of which is the performance of the company. The biggest influence of all is usually the general direction of the market as a whole, which exerts pressure on all shares. A lasting bull market will eventually push up the price of even a mediocre company's shares while a bear market, conversely, will depress the share price of the very best company. But these observations cover the longer term. What about weekly, or even daily price movements? Why can a company's shares sometimes move by as much as 5% in 24 hours when the company itself has issued no news?

What about the yield on the shares, or the ratio of their price to the company's profits? And the directors who buy and sell, not to mention the highly paid analysts who are employed by stockbrokers to keep an eye on the company within its sector of the market. Any one of them may decide to recommend a switch into another share in the same sector and the resulting weight of institutional orders will exert pressure on both of these.

Over the years much work goes into studying the company itself. There is an argument that the share price at any one time reflects all known facts. But of course this does not allow for the third dimension: human behaviour. Many psychological factors are at work to move the price of a share but at the core of my argument is that the price you or I paid for a share influences our subsequent actions.

We all remember what price we paid for our house, the car, the holiday, our lunch – and of course the shares we have bought. If the price of the shares we have just bought falls, we breathe a sigh of relief when it gets back to the price we paid. If the fall has been a sharp one we may be tempted to sell as soon as we get a chance to retrieve our original investment stake. Similarly, if we have taken a profit on a share which subsequently falls, we might be very tempted indeed to buy again when our original purchase price is reached again, in the hope of repeating the exercise.

Just imagine the powers at work when, during a busy period in the market, thousands of investors have all dealt around the same price. That price will have considerable significance for some time to come. So you should be aware of it. It could pay to know where the supply tap might be switched on, exerting downward pressure on the price, or where buyers may begin to operate again.

The technical terms for these levels are "support" and "resistance" and references to these will be found throughout this book. They are one of the prime keys to understanding charting and to using it to your advantage.

The study of price movements has become quite a sophisticated art. And an art it certainly is. Not a science. But it remains shrouded in mystery to many investors who are sceptical that price changes can be recorded and worthwhile conclusions drawn from them. Even some financial journalists are quick to criticise because they have a misconception that charting is merely about past price movements repeating themselves. But this is only a very small part of the story.

TWO

THE BASIC PRINCIPLES

Having established that you want to keep a track of price movements, a decision has to be made on how best to do it. Most of us remember our maths lessons at school and the sort of simple graphs we used to draw. By

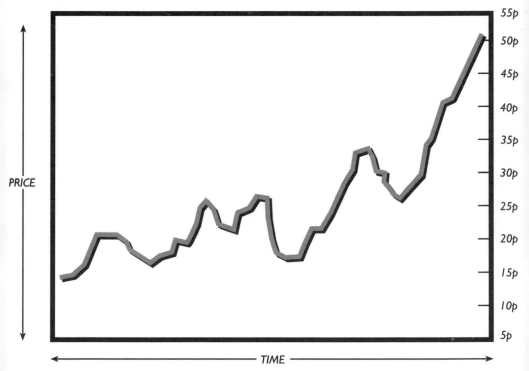

Figure 1: A simple price and time chart.

having time move along one axis and price moving up and down the other we can join together daily, or weekly, price changes to form a curve.

It will be most common for us to use ordinary squared paper where every square is the same size as the one next to it. This is called *arithmetic* paper and is available from any good drawing office. So it is easy to get started. A simple chart, plotting, say, the closing price each day from the newspaper over a period of time. An example is given in *Figure 1* on page 13.

We can, of course, use different information. For instance, if the data is available to us, we could plot the day's highest and lowest prices at which shares have changed hands, joining these with a vertical bar. Let's say that a share has been dealt in at prices throughout the day of 48p, 50p, 49p, 50p again and 51p. The day's highest price is therefore 51p and the lowest 48p. This is known as the day's **range** and is shown below in *Figure 2*.

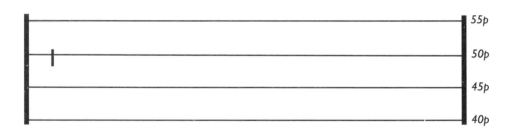

Figure 2: A day's price range.

The bars representing the daily range will accumulate over a period of time and build to produce the classic **bar chart** as shown in *Figure 3* on page 15.

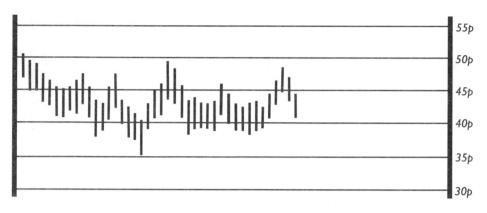

Figure 3: A bar chart.

For additional information in the picture we could add a short horizontal bar to represent the closing price of the day as shown below in *Figure 4*.

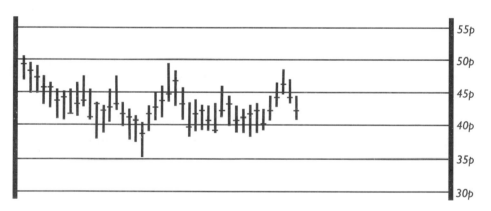

Figure 4: A bar chart with closing prices.

To this chart could be added the number of shares traded during each day; this is commonly referred to as **volume.** This information can be obtained for the leading shares in the market from quality daily newspapers, and certainly the *Financial Times*. Our chart will now look as drawn in *Figure 5* on page 16.

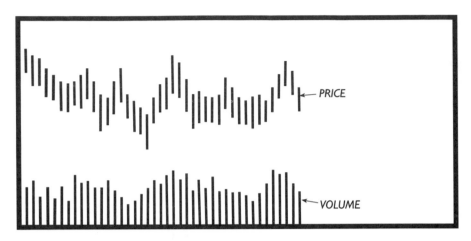

Figure 5: A bar chart with price and volume.

The reasons for plotting volume on the charts will be discussed later but it is convenient to plot it as a vertical bar. Doing this keeps the chart uncluttered to the eye; we have more information to overlay on the chart later and must leave space for this. You'll soon become used to volume plotted in this way and it's a standard adopted by chartists all over the world.

Reverting for a moment to the grid which has been used so far, the big problem with arithmetically scaled chart paper is that the further a price moves the faster it appears to go. This is an illusion.

Let's take the example of a chart which is given a scale of 5p per square. A movement of one square when the share price stands at 50p will represent a 10% move. But a move of one square at 500p, which takes up the same space on the chart, represents a move of just 1%. Or put another way, a move of 10% in the price at 50p will cover only one square but a move of similar proportions will cover 10 squares at 500p. This is illustrated in *Figure 6* on page 17.

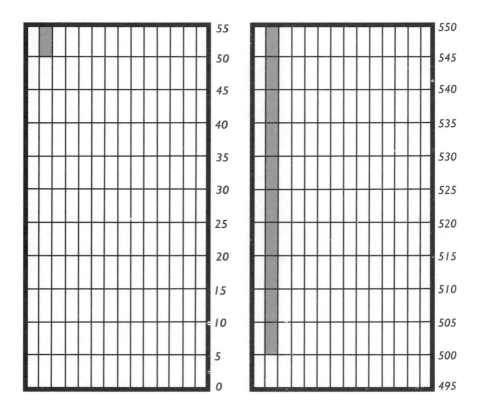

Figure 6: The illusion of % movements.

We can overcome this phenomenon by using *logarithmic* graph paper. Don't be put off by this throwback to your school days. It's quite simple really. With log paper the squares get smaller and smaller as you go up the scale:

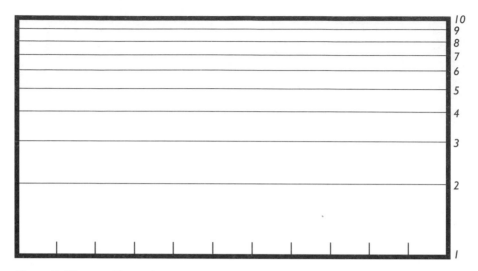

Figure 7: The use of logarithmic graph paper.

The use of log paper rids us of the illusion of a price seeming to move faster and faster the higher it goes. No matter where the price is plotted on log paper a move of, say, 10% is going to take up the same amount of space. Measure it for yourself in *Figure 7* above and you will see that a move from 2 to 4 is going to take the same space as a move from 4 to 8. Both of these moves are 100%.

An important thing to remember with single cycle log paper like this is that the price at the top of the scale will always be 10 times the price at the bottom. I can well remember when I first started using log paper and I didn't appreciate this. And because the top is 10 times the bottom, **the chart cannot start with zero** .

Because successful investment is a percentage game it helps to keep moves in proportion. For this reason all my *investment* charts are maintained on log paper. All my *trading* charts – for tracking short-term movements in traded option stocks, for instance – are kept on ordinary arithmetic paper in order to exaggerate movements and put them under the microscope.

Very short-term traders in the currency and futures markets use much expanded arithmetic scales. This is because they are frequently dealing on very small price movements and need to put a magnifier on both the price action and the timescale. I've seen traders on the floor of the Mercantile Exchange in Chicago keeping minute-to-minute charts on small pads of graph paper. They need to maintain a feel for small price movements because they frequently trade several times a morning in the same commodity or financial contract. But in this book we will confine ourselves to daily and weekly plotted charts which are likely to help you most with timing the purchases and sales of stocks and shares.

Try plotting a series of price movements for yourself. The first decision, and sometimes the most difficult, is to decide on the scale you are going to use. If the scale is too narrow you will lose the desired detail. Make the scale too wide and there will appear to be so much movement that it will be difficult to interpret what you see. Take the FT-SE 100 Index (or Footsie as it is familiarly known) over a one month period.

This is one of the easiest exercises to complete because you will find the FT-SE 100 Index closing figure in almost every national and major regional newspaper. You can also obtain it from CEEFAX and Teletext financial pages on your TV set. I have completed a tabulation for you on page 20.

The FT-SE 100 Index daily closes were as follows during August 1994:

DATE	PRICE
Monday 1st	3097.4
Tuesday 2nd	3157.5
Wednesday 3rd	3160.4
Thursday 4th	3150.5
Friday 5th	3167.5
Monday 8th	3171.9
Tuesday 9th	3168.6
Wednesday 10th	3167.0
Thursday 11th	3138.2
Friday 12th	3142.3
Monday 15th	3142.2
Tuesday 16th	3147.3
Wednesday 17th	3190.3
Thursday 18th	3182.6
Friday 19th	3191.4
Monday 22nd	3171.3
Tuesday 23rd	3175.1
Wednesday 24th	3205.2
Thursday 25th	3234.2
Friday 26th	3265.1
Monday 29th	Bank Holiday
Tuesday 30th	3249.6
Wednesday 31st	3251.3

The range of movement is about 150 points. So we should choose a scale for the chart which is going to be suitable. For argument's sake we will decide on 10 points per square. Now put these on a piece of graph paper, joining up the daily closing levels to produce a curve:

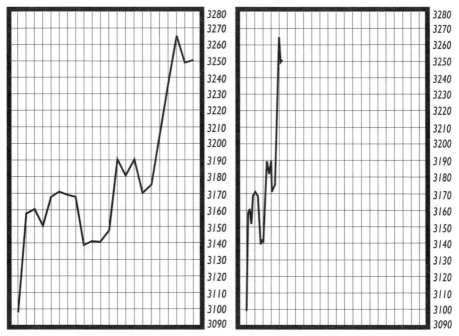

Figure 8a: 1 square = 1 day.   *Figure 8b: 1 square = 1 week.*

A timescale has also to be chosen. A single square could represent a day, a week or a month, for instance. *Figure 8a* above is plotted on the basis of 1 square = 1 day while the chart in *Figure 8b* is 1 square = 1 week. In the latter case you are going to have to fit in five plots into the square and will need good eyesight. Believe me, you will get used to doing this quite quickly with practice. The advantage of such a tight timescale is that your chart will cover a longer period of time, giving greater perspective. And it will take longer before it runs off the end of the paper and you have to redraw, or tack on some more grid. It all depends on your own timescale for your investments.

Of course in this modern day and age there are many cheap computer charting packages available. Their advantages are considerable as you can flick from arithmetic to logarithmic charts in an instant and the machine will automatically choose a price scale to fit the grid. They save a lot of time and are immensely flexible (see Chapter 7).

Whatever method you employ for keeping your charts, you will first of all be looking for a price **trend** which will tell you the main **direction** of price movements. Such trends, it will be discovered, can last for quite long periods of time. And quite simply it is going to pay you to follow the trend until it stops. As the saying goes, "the trend is your friend". This may sound trite but the more you use it the more likely you are to be a successful investor.

You should be aware that experience has shown that a trend is valid only when it has three points or more of contact; only two points mean that it is too fragile to base an investment decision upon. A typical trend in a rising market might look like this; you will notice that it is made up of a number of rises which have been interrupted by various setbacks:

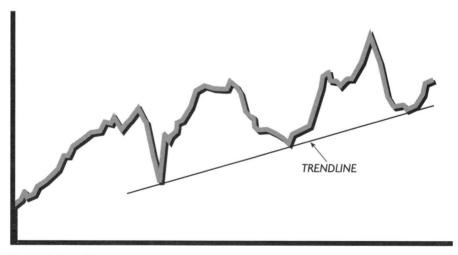

Figure 9: Trendline.

While the trend stays in the same direction you must not fight it. The key to investment success is your *strategy*. In a bull market you must buy on setbacks such as those in *Figure 9* on page 22 as your expectation is that prices will continue rising again after these pauses. In a bear market the opposite applies; you should sell on rallies in price as the trend tells you that lower prices will follow in due course . Thus if you were able to discover when the trend is changing you could – and indeed *should* – change your strategy.

And eventually there will come a time when a trend will stop, as sure as night follows day. No share, not even that of the most successful and fast-growing company, will go on rising without interruption. And all bear markets come to an end. However, some shares do carry on falling while the company goes bust but such cases are extremely rare.

At this point I ought to mention the strangely-titled 'Point and Figure' and 'Candlestick' charting techniques. They are both popular and you should be aware of them.

At first sight they are strange to look at but they do have their respective advantages. In the case of the *Point and Figure* chart (*Figure 10* on page 24) the action is condensed in order to omit price changes which are regarded as too small to be of significance, or periods when the price fails to change at all. There is no timescale. The chart is plotted only when the price changes by a predetermined amount.

It may look like a spot-the-ball competition entry but the convention is that rising prices are represented by Xs and falling prices by Os. Sometimes time is represented by putting in a month number for the first plot that particular month, instead of the X or O.

The chart is plotted in vertical columns, and only changes if the price moves outside the box in which it was last plotted. The aim of this is to highlight the important trading and thus identify significant levels. It ignores any tight sideways trading, which is regarded as irrelevant.

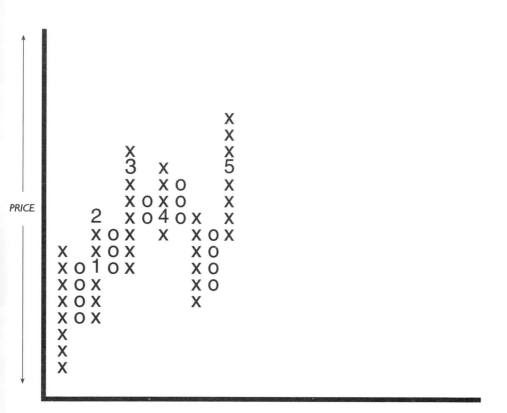

Figure 10: Point and Figure

I have used this kind of chart in the past but one of the big problems in modern times is that, because of their lack of a timescale, they do not allow any additional information to be included so that you are making your decisions only on the patterns which build up (see next chapter). None of the additional indicators, dealt with later in this book, can be used. This, I find, is a significant drawback although I still know of some very successful exponents of the technique, particularly David Fuller, a well-known analyst and news-letter writer in London. I will stop here but further reading can be done and details are contained in the bibliography in Appendix One on page 151.

Candlestick charts have become popular in recent years. They originated in Japan where they are used almost exclusively by locals. Now that westerners have taken the trouble to learn about them, they are seen more often in City dealing rooms. The name 'Candlestick' comes from the shape of the plots, although I personally would have thought that 'Candle' would be more accurate. Perhaps something got lost in the translation.

To plot these charts you need the day's opening, highest, lowest and closing prices. The highest and lowest prices are joined together with a vertical bar just as I have described earlier in this chapter. To complete the candlestick chart, draw in a horizontal line protruding either side of the bar to represent the closing price and another for the opening price, as in *Figure 11a* below. Then join the edges of the horizontal lines as in *Figure 11b* below. If the closing price of the day was above the opening price of the day, the body of the candle is left white. Conversely, if the price closed lower than it opened, the body is shaded black.

Figure 11a: Candlestick construction.   *Figure 11b: Completed Candlestick.*

A chart plotted over a period of time will look like this:

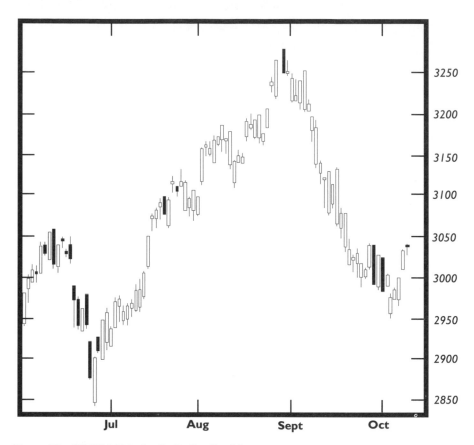

Figure 11c: FT-SE 100 Index Daily Candlesticks.

Thus, once you become accustomed to using them, candlesticks give you considerable information. And they have their own analysis techniques, too, in addition to many of those described in this book.

The problem for the private investor is in getting hold of the Open/High/Low/Close prices in order to plot the chart in the first place! Most newspapers just don't report them all. For this reason I will stop at this point but if you do have access to the information, probably on a 'Reuter' or similar system, I would recommend that you do some more work on this aspect of charting. Suitable reading is listed in the bibliography contained in Appendix One on page 151.

THREE

CONTINUATION PATTERNS

No price goes in the same direction indefinitely. Investors take profits, or delay their purchases, if they believe that the price has risen too sharply or if the background to the market looks shaky. This leads to setbacks, commonly known as consolidations, or reactions, which combine to form *continuation patterns* on the chart.

It is a fact that prices spend the bulk of the time thinking where to go and considerably less time actually getting there. As an investor it is important that your money is working for you and you don't want to hold shares which are not going to move. But if you are holding a share whose price suffers one of these setbacks, for instance, there is very little point in selling if the price is going to start rising again soon.

If you don't yet own any shares in the company, it may be better to delay a purchase until there are definite signs that the price is moving ahead again. Within the context of an overall trend there can be many important opportunities for you to get on board and make profits.

Continuation patterns repeat themselves again and again. They are not always regular in shape, however, and the beginner can find them difficult to recognise in practice. Chartists give them unfamiliar names for ease of reference and these are universally used in the marketplace. But the names need not concern you too much at this stage. More important is to build up your powers of recognition; if opportunities are going to present themselves you will stand a better chance of getting your timing right if you know what to look for.

Continuation patterns last for varying periods of time. Most will develop over a period of weeks or months but some will last only a matter of days in very active and powerfully moving markets.

Let's look at some of the most common continuation patterns:

The Triangle

The rationale behind the development of the triangle pattern is that a battle is going on between buyers and sellers. Triangles can have flat tops, (*Figure 12a,* below). Sometimes they are more regular, with two sloping sides (*Figure 12b,* below):

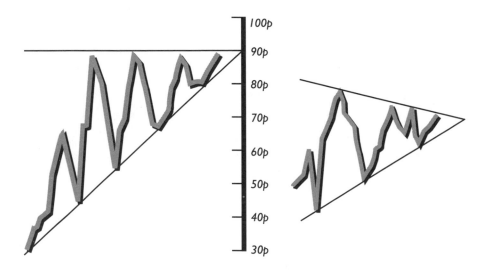

Figure 12a: Flat top.   *Figure 12b: Sloping sides.*

In *Figure 12a* on the previous page, the top is flat because sellers are persistent at 90p. At that price they believe the shares are fully valued and they dispose of shares each time the price reaches it. The buyers, meanwhile, are growing increasingly impatient and are putting in their orders at higher and higher prices. So a convergence of opinion develops. Eventually one side will get the upper hand as the other's orders run dry and the price breaks out of the triangle. This is where the chart becomes interesting. A sharp, potentially profitable, move is now very likely to occur. The knowledge that it is happening can give you an edge over other investors and is therefore very valuable to you.

There are a number of useful features of the triangle pattern you should understand. The more points of contact that the sides of the triangle have with the price, the better and more reliable the pattern becomes. But as a minimum *there should be three points of contact on each*. Triangles do build up with fewer than this but the degree of validity of the pattern increases with three.

However, experience has shown that *the closer to the apex, or point, of the triangle the price gets, the less reliable the pattern becomes.* The best results come from breaks which occur at between the halfway and three-quarters points. I have never understood why this should be but over the years I have learned that once the three-quarters mark has been passed it is better to place less emphasis on the pattern and look for something else to do.

One of the benefits of charting techniques is that they give you a target price to work on. As shown in *Figure 13* on page 32, by measuring the depth of the triangle at the beginning of its formation (a - b), we can project this measurement onto the point of breakout (c - d).

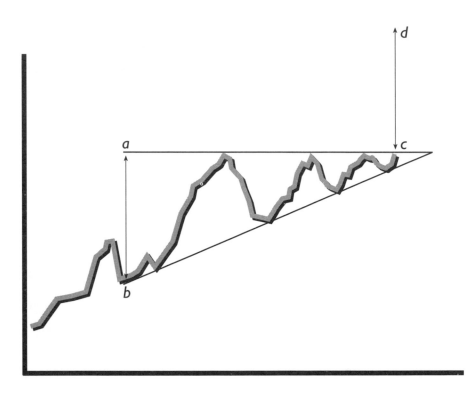

Figure 13: Target pricing.

This now gives a working target for the price. At such a point short-term traders may wish to take a profit. Longer term investors will use it as a confirmation that the price is conforming to basic charting rules and should eventually move higher again, perhaps after some further hesitation. You will certainly be building up a 'feel' for the way the share is behaving.

The Rectangle

This is a rather less common pattern than the triangle but it occurs for much the same reasons. However it is clear from the shape that a two-way argument between buyers and sellers is occurring between distinct battle lines. In *Figure 14* below, the sellers are feeding shares to the market just above 60p while the price is being supported by buying orders at 55p. The rectangle builds up as the price hits the top time and again until the sellers become exhausted and the buyers gain the upper hand. The price then moves swiftly through the vacuum which has built up above the top of the pattern.

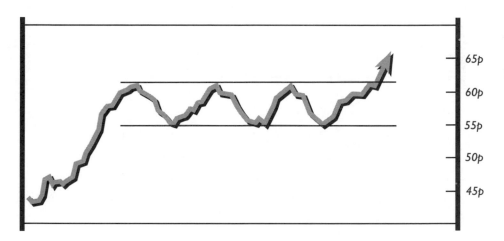

Figure 14: The Rectangle.

Occasionally there is a temporary setback - the chartist jargon is a 'pull-back' – as a late seller appears on the scene; this is usually a second chance to buy if you miss the pattern first time. It is rarely a permanent problem if you have already bought on the first upward break. It is shown in *Figure 15* on page 34.

Rectangles typically build up over a number of months and it is by no means uncommon for them to last for over a year. So you have to be patient and bide your time. Sometimes the sheer timespan of the pattern will lead to your taking your eye off it; this is where a pullback can be a useful second chance to do something.

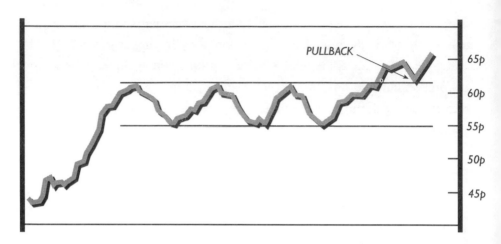

Figure 15: Pullback.

As with the triangle, we can measure a working target. Take the depth of the rectangle (a - b) and project it upwards from the point of breakout (c - d) to give yourself a minimum working target. This is demonstrated in *Figure 16* below.

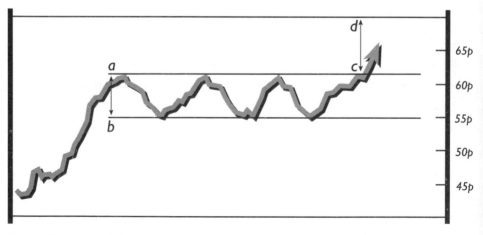

Figure 16: Target pricing.

The Flag

Flags, or pennants as they are sometimes known, are tight little consolidations, or hesitations in price and occur over very short periods of time – from a few days to three weeks. They are associated with fast moving situations and will happen after a steep rise has taken place. The rise itself takes on the appearance of a flagpole, hence the name given to the consolidation. A typical example may look like this:-

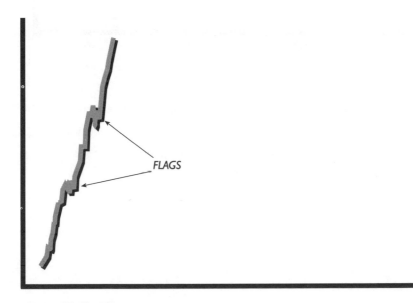

Figure 17: The Flag.

However, flags can come in all shapes. It takes practice to recognise them and they won't show up at all if the scale on your chart is too tight. They can be very irregular in shape and sometimes, in the case of those which develop over only a few days, have no real "shape" at all. An example is given in *Figure 18* on page 36.

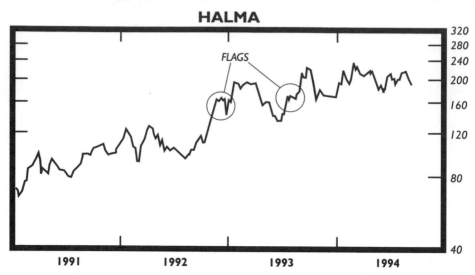

Figure 18: Flags.

Once again there exists a measuring technique. Take the length of the immediately preceding sharp rise within the flagpole (a - b) and project this upwards from the point of the break from the flag pattern (c - d) to give the immediate minimum target. *Figure 19* below shows this.

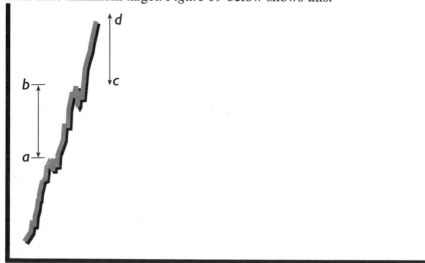

Figure 19: Target pricing.

Remember, however, that if such a pattern has persisted for more than four weeks it is unlikely to be a true flag. It is much more likely to develop into one of the other continuation patterns.

Incidentally, I know of one successful trader who only deals on breaks from flags. His argument is that this pattern, coming only as part of explosive price moves, is going to give the chance of quick profits. He also knows very soon if it is going wrong. The pattern is going to fail if the break occurs and then does not follow through as expected. If the price falls below where the flag began to form, a loss can be taken quickly without too much damage.

Get to know and recognise these key continuation patterns with practice. They occur all the time and can be very helpful to your strategy and tactics whether you are a short-term trader or a longer term investor.

FOUR

REVERSAL PATTERNS

It is a fact that all trends will come to an end. No market will go on rising, or falling, for ever. It is essential that you have a way of recognising such change, as this is the time when you need to change your strategy. In bull markets you should buy into dips but in bear markets you ought to sell into rallies. Knowing what kind of market you are operating in is vital to your financial well being.

Price charts very frequently display recognisable characteristics at times of trend change. There are patterns which can alert you to the transition. They won't get you out of the market at the top, nor in at the bottom, but they can save your profit when things are beginning to go wrong, or alert you when a seemingly never-ending bear market is coming to an end. These are the times when fundamental, or traditional, methods of analysis will usually let you down.

At the bottom of a bearish phase in the market the economic news is almost certain to be bad; witness, for instance, the market at the time of the sterling crisis in 1992. The news was appaling but the market took off from that point and went on to rise by almost 50% over the next 16 months.

Similarly, at the end of 1993 when the FT-SE Index rose above 3,500 it was widely believed that it would go higher still; inflation was out of the system for good and interest rates would go on falling. But now we all know that a hike in US rates frightened the markets into a damaging fall of almost 17% in 6 months from the beginning of 1994.

Classical reversal patterns will help you identify these turning points. They have been given names which cause a lot of amusement on the part of commentators who don't understand charting. They are nevertheless descriptive of their shapes. With practice you will learn to recognise them and, eventually, to ignore them at your peril.

Double Top

Do you remember what I was saying earlier about the price you paid for a share sticking in your mind? It is quite a natural reaction for us to look to get our money back if the price of a share falls after we have bought it and a subsequent rally takes place. We have had a scare and perhaps have begun to question our original reasons for buying it in the first place. If a number of investors begin to think this way the pressures to sell at a price can build into an irresistible force.

In the case of a double top, this is precisely what happens – see *Figure 20* on page 41. The share price reaches a high point and then falls away. After a while (a few months normally) buyers come back to dominate the market for a while but are unable to force the price through the old peak. The price drops again and eventually cuts through the level from which the previous rally had developed. Think of this pattern as a letter 'M' and you will remember it. The price penetrating the mid-point of the 'M' is your signal to sell.

The double top is a relatively common occurrence and its message should not be ignored. It is a bearish signal. Admittedly one of its shortcomings is that it will not get you out at the top but then how many methods are there to guarantee this? At least it instils the discipline on you to do something and get out while the going is good.

As with the continuation patterns we have looked at earlier there is a measuring technique for you to use in order to arrive at a minimum target price; but do remember that it is a minimum and the price may well fall further. Once the target is reached you may wish to reconsider your position but at least you are out when the price is falling.

The mid-point of the 'M' pattern is the support. This is known as the 'neckline' - another piece of jargon for you to remember, I'm afraid. In order to use a measuring technique to arrive at the minimum target you take the distance between the peak in price and this neckline (a - b). You then project this measurement down from the neckline (c - d)

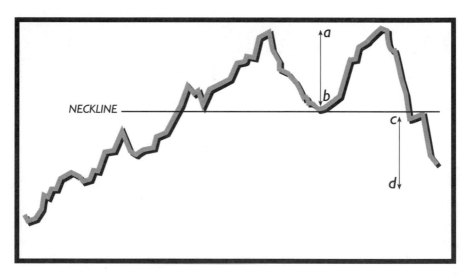

Figure 20: A Double Top.

It will be observed that the neckline in this case is horizontal. In fact, this is unusual as most necklines will have a tilt. Most bearish are the ones which slope from left to right. This is because a low right shoulder will indicate that the fall has already begun.

A mirror of the double top occurs at the bottom of a fall when the market in the share has been weak; not unsurprisingly this is known as the 'double bottom': *Figure 21* on page 42. The psychology of the pattern is similar. In this case the sellers have driven the price down to a level which attracts some buyers and a rally takes place. Other investors take notice that profits are being made in the share again but do not feel inclined to chase the price upwards.

For any number of reasons the price falls back again but only to the support level at the earlier low. Those who have bought there last time have

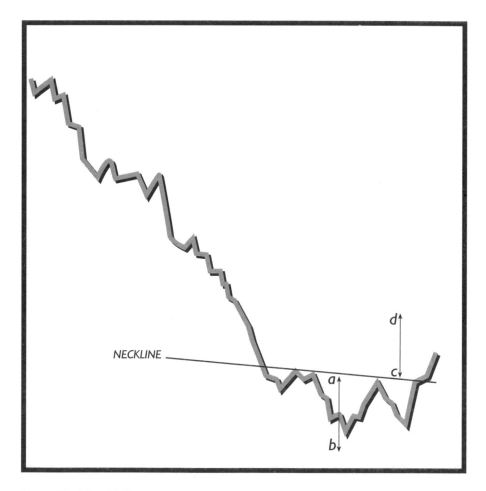

Figure 21: A Double Bottom.

seen their investment make a good profit and are tempted to repeat the exercise while those who failed to buy last time are now willing to support the price at, or around its low. The price bounces again and, because this time the profit takers don't appear, it rises through the old resistance level. The double bottom pattern is completed and there is now a very strong buy signal which could turn out to be profitable.

Again the measuring technique comes in. In a mirror image of the double top, the minimum expected rise is a repeat (c - d) of the distance between the lows and the neckline (a - b). And again remember that this is a minimum working target. As in *Figure 15* on page 34, a pullback can occur.

Head and Shoulders

The strangely titled 'head and shoulders' has been the subject of much derision from the uninformed. Jokes about shampoo abound. I would advise the newcomer to forget about the name but learn to recognise the pattern as it is pretty reliable - and thus potentially profitable.

The head and shoulders top builds up after the price has been in a steady uptrend for some time and many investors hold shares which stand them at a profit. The price rises until profit taking sets in and a plateau builds up. Then there is a further rise which takes the price to a new high but this becomes unsustainable, for reasons which are rarely apparent at the time. The price falls away but buyers gain the upper hand and a rally gets underway. Only this time the price fails to get back to the previous peak and sellers begin to dominate the market.

The price now settles at a similar level to the earlier setback but after a time it is unable to rise as it did the previous time and the support level is tested and gives way. This support level is again called the 'neckline' and assumes great importance.

The breaking of the neckline is not something which should be ignored.

It has been shown to be one of the more reliable of the signals which charts can give. Studies by statisticians have proved that it works in the majority of cases.

Again a measuring technique comes into use as shown in *Figure 22* below. Take the distance, a - b, between the top of the price (the 'head') and the neckline (the 'shoulder') and project it downwards to give a minimum working target for the price to fall to, c - d :

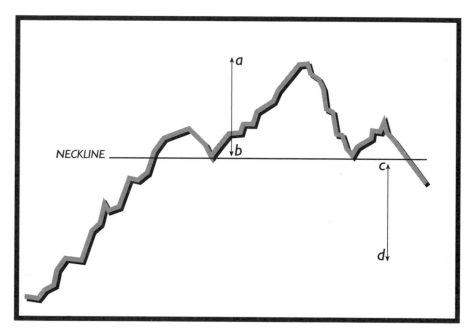

Figure 22: Target pricing.

It will perhaps not surprise you to learn that in a bear market the head and shoulders top has a mirror image at the bottom. The technical term for it is the 'reverse head and shoulders' and it is shown in *Figure 23* on page 45. Again there is the measuring technique to help reach a working target.

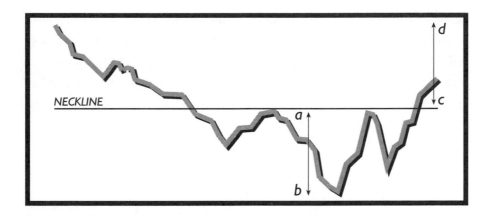

Figure 23: Reverse Head and Shoulders.

Rounding, or Saucer, Tops and Bottoms

The very names here tell you what the patterns are going to look like. They are less dramatic than the spiky Double Tops and Bottoms or Head and Shoulders patterns.

Saucer tops build up over time and reflect maturing bull markets which are very slowly changing their characteristics. There is no panic during their formation and the sellers' orders are more or less absorbed by the buyers. But the price drifts slowly into a turn with selling pressure constantly building.

At the bottom of a bear market, the opposite phenomenon occurs. Buying pressure slowly builds as gradually more and more investors decide to put a toe in the water; the result is the Saucer Bottom.

Sometimes the patterns formed at tops and bottoms do not *precisely* conform to those which I have described but you will learn to adapt as you become more experienced.

Take, for instance, the multiple top which built up in the shares of

Betterware in 1993, *Figure 24* below. The company will be known to you as the one which sends catalogues of household products through your letterbox, followed a few days later by someone who calls to take your order. This is a modification of the man with the suitcase full of brushes, polish etc. who used to come round in my childhood. The new sales tactic took off in a big way a few years ago and the shares became the stockmarket's darlings, rising almost vertically over several years.

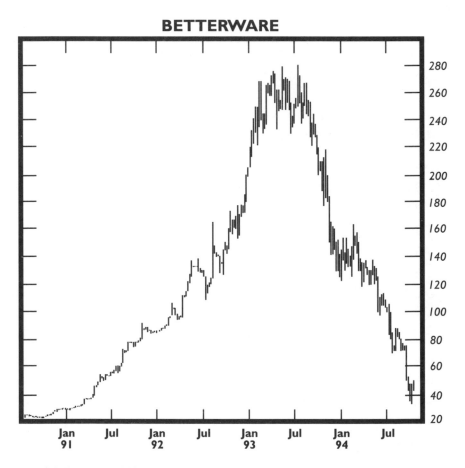

Figure 24: Betterware 1991 – 1994.

But then suddenly they stalled at 280p; try as they might, they just couldn't get above that level. Many attempts were made during early 1993 but it became apparent to the chart watcher that something important was happening. Was it a rectangle consolidation area or was something more sinister going on? The news was still bullish – the company was to expand into France, selling its wares to Pierre and Genevieve. But still the sellers of the shares were persistent.

Eventually the very important support for the shares at 230p dried up and a steep fall began. The company knew of no reason. The market analysts knew of none either.

But the situation had changed. And the relative strength line at the bottom of the chart had started to fall, too (see Chapter 5). Within 6 months the price had crashed to 125p, less than half the level of a year earlier. At the time of writing this chapter, the shares were down to 74p following an announcement that the new warehousing system had been poor and that sales were beginning to fall. And France was not going at all well. Yet another case of the market knowing best.

Whether you would call the pattern a saucer, or rounding top or whether it is just a nameless multiple top, is debatable. But without doubt it is recognisable as a top of some significance, with confirmation from the relative strength curve.

What about Next *Figure 25* on page 48, the riches to rags story of the troubled High Street retailer? From its humble beginnings as Hepworths, the tailors, the company was guided by George Davis to become a highly successful retailer of fashions. But then it all started to go wrong and the story ended in acrimony as Mr Davis lost his job and the company pruned and cut away at itself in order to ensure its own survival. The price of the shares was down to a couple of pence from a high of 360p only a few years earlier.

Certainly the chart was not telling us anything positive at all but a sharp

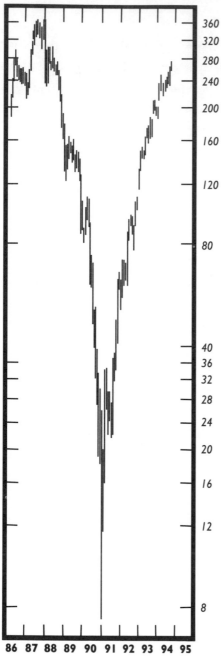

Figure 25: Next 1986 – 1994.

bounce over several months began to produce the reversal pattern which strongly suggested that recovery might be underway. A deep head and shoulders reversal was confirmed by a move through the neckline at 34p; at the time of writing, the shares stand at many times that price.

So here we have studied some of the clear reversal patterns which occur at market tops and bottoms. Learn to recognise them and they will help you to keep your profits, or at worst cut your losses, ahead of a price fall. And in reverse they can alert you to a changing situation after a market fall and lead you to at least having a long look at a company whose 'bombed out' share price may be changing for the better.

I know of no other way of spotting key turning points. Looking at the company's accounts certainly won't alert you to a change in market sentiment. But looking at a change in market sentiment may alert you to a change in the company's accounts! The evidence behind the change in sentiment will only appear later - when it is too late to sell or buy at a good price. I have seen this so many times I could write a book about it! Here is just one example.

Polly Peck became one of the stockmarket's darlings a few years ago. From small beginnings as a hosiery manufacturer the company grew under Asil Nadir's stewardship to produce packaging and televisions in Cyprus and Turkey. Eventually it grew so big in stockmarket terms that it was able to take over Del Monte, the fruit canners and became a constituent of the FT-SE 100 Index. What subsequently happened is still a matter for the receivers and the courts to settle.

From a matter of just a few pence the shares rose and rose to reach a peak at 460p. The chart was superb and the penny share tipsters were heavily promoting the great success story in the national press.

But suddenly the chart took a turn for the worse. The evidence was growing that the shares were running out of buyers who were prepared to support it. We didn't know why, but to the chart watcher the collapse below 375p in the middle of August 1990 was drastic. The tight little 'flag' pattern which then built up over 4 days was the last signal to get out, particularly as the relative strength curve had collapsed too (see the next chapter).

The message was clear that the time had come to sell. Subsequently the news broke that all was not well with the company and the price crashed through the support at 200p. This is shown in *Figure 26* on page 50.

No form of fundamental analysis would have got you out of this disaster. Not even the company's accountants had uncovered the truth – whatever it was. But fortunes were lost and many investors rued the day they were caught.

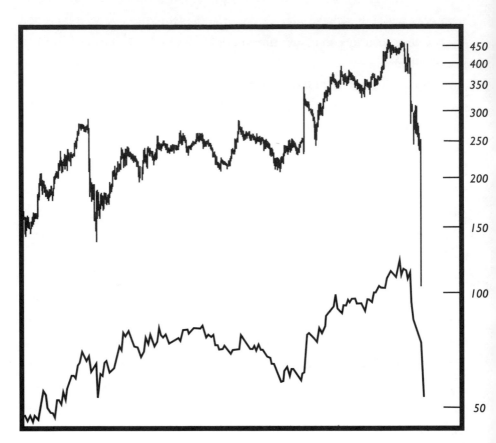

Figure 26: Polly Peck International 1988-90.

I admit that this is an extreme case but similar, less dramatic cases are legion. The charts in many – not all – instances have provided warning signals of a shift in sentiment well before real trouble is obvious from other sources.

It is the share which falls like a stone that damages your portfolio badly, to the extent that you have to find some big winners to make up the shortfall. Happily such falls are relatively uncommon but if the chart says 'sell' then you should take avoiding action. Or suffer the consequences, however small or great they may be.

A word of warning is appropriate here. You will see *potential* reversal patterns building on your charts very frequently and it is vital that you do not jump the gun. What appears to be a threatening double top, for instance, may go on to develop into a rectangle. You must *never* act upon a potential pattern until it is completed. At times you will be furious that you could have dealt earlier at a better price but I can tell you from my own experience that the premature deals are the ones which cost you the most money in the longer run.

Wait for the pattern to develop fully and never try to second guess the outcome.

FIVE

MATHEMATICAL INDICATORS

One of the problems with the standard patterns which I have described is that they are not 100% reliable. This should come as no surprise to anybody, of course, otherwise those "in the know" would be quietly making their fortunes and I would not be sitting here writing this book. But what I really mean is that there is a larger margin of error when patterns are acted upon in isolation. So we require a filtering mechanism which cuts down the mistakes to a more profitable level. By overlaying extra indicators to confirm the patterns we can hopefully increase the success rate.

Mathematical calculations abound. There is no shortage of experts who have invented various ratios and conducted momentum studies to unlock the mysteries of how prices move. The advent of the computer in recent years has made possible all sorts of complicated formulae.

So where do you, the private investor begin? And are the mathematics going to be beyond your understanding? Well, I would by no means describe myself as a mathematician but I get by with my old 'O' level maths and don't need to remember the algebra and geometry to do so.

In my experience of the last 25 years or so, using secondary, or additional, indicators does cut down the error rate considerably. However, I know many people in the fund management and currency markets who swear by the various different tools which they use.

My conclusion is that you should familiarise yourself with several of them by using them over a period of time and then let your own experience dictate which ones you feel most comfortable with. Over the years I have used many indicators; some have been discarded along the way for having let me down at important moments while others have become trusted friends without whom my investment decisions would be very much poorer.

Relative Strength

One to start off with is relative strength. It is simple to calculate and will set you in the right direction. It is a checking mechanism for you to tell whether your shares are outperforming or underperforming the market. Thus you can weed out those which are not earning their keep and concentrate on those which are doing better than the market.

In a general bull market, for instance, a share price might rise under the influence of the overall direction of prices, pulled upwards by a general market re-rating. But this might mask an underlying hidden weakness and when the time comes for the market as a whole to take a rest you may find that such a share begins to fall quite sharply. I've seen it happen many times.

How can you monitor this performance? The easy way is to calculate the relative strength of the share each day, or once a week. To do this you take the share price and divide it by the market index you have chosen to use.

The FT-Actuaries All-Share Index should be your choice – it's widely quoted and representative of most shares as it is constructed from over 800 of the largest ones quoted. Then take, for example, Marks & Spencer. On Monday 3rd October 1994 the shares stood at 398.5p at the close of business for the day. The All-Share Index closed at 1490.83. By taking out your calculator (you won't need a computer for this one) and dividing the share price by the All-Share Index you will get a figure, 26.73. This is the ratio of the share price to the market, known as relative strength.

If you then repeat the calculation every week for a period of time, the results will begin to look something like this when plotted on your chart:-

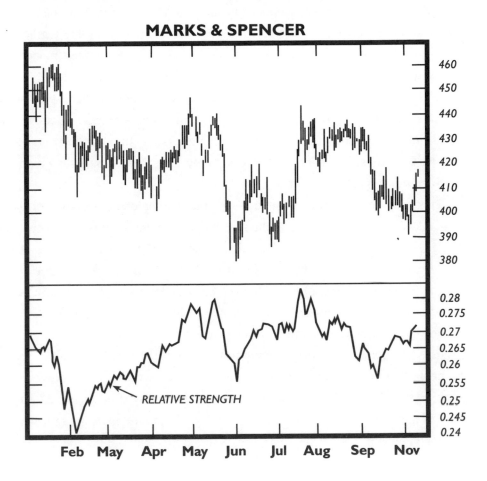

MARKS & SPENCER

Figure 27: Relative Strength.

On this chart the upper line is the plot of the price and the lower one is our relative strength curve. Rising relative strength means that the share is *outperforming* the market while, conversely, *falling* relative strength shows a share *underperforming* the market. Rarely will any share consistently behave exactly the same as the market but if it did, of course, the relative strength plots would be flat, or sideways moving. But it is more normal for shares to enjoy periods of outperforming and underperforming the market and, for the reasons I have described earlier, it will help you to make money if you are able to identify changes of direction in relative strength.

You should look initially for a trend which has developed over a period of time. Experience shows that relative strength or weakness can sometimes persist for long periods. Indeed, my firm plots relative strength on its very long-term charts and it is interesting to see how long these trends can go on for. Sometimes it can be for years.

This long-term picture identifies the underlying characteristics of a share. Compare the lower line on the two charts on page 57; it is the relative strength plotted over a 7-year period. Just look how flat the performance of GEC is when compared with the volatility of British Aerospace. It will help you to know that one (BAe) is much more fast moving than the other as it is an indication of the amount of risk your investment is likely to involve.

For the shorter term picture, as with the trends in price which I have discussed earlier, you need as many points of contact between the plots on the chart and your trend line, and certainly at least three. Let's draw in some on the chart of Marks and Spencer which was used in *Figure 27* on page 55 and it will be seen in *Figure 29* on page 58 that relative strength can develop in phases. The Spring of 1994 saw the shares outstripping the market until the setback in early May, whereas they distinctly underperformed from mid-July to early September. Plainly if you are a short-term operator, in the fast moving Traded Options market for instance, it pays to know when a share is going to do better or worse than the market. If you can find the fastest movers you will make bigger profits.

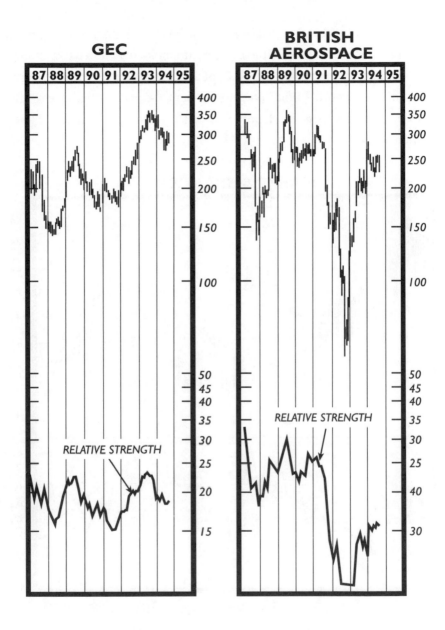

Figure 28: Relative Strength charts.

If you are a longer term investor, you will need a longer term chart than this and consequently you will get different results on the relative strength curve; the short-term trends just described will be scarcely visible. But the same principles apply. If your portfolio contains shares with above average relative strength, you must perform better than the market. That is common sense.

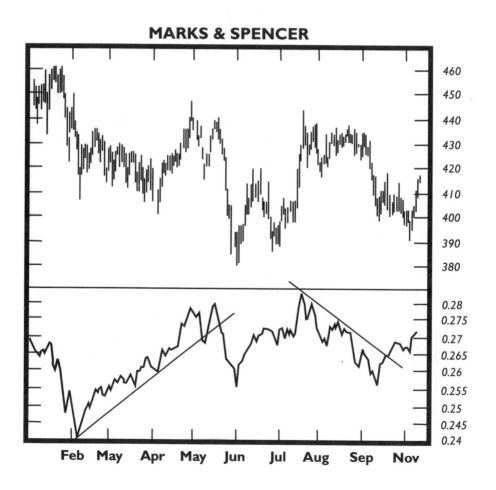

Figure 29: Relative strength trends.

A change in trend on the relative strength curve may be a warning signal that something is changing in the share price itself. A share which has been consistently outperforming the market but then begins to lag may just be taking a breather but something more sinister may be afoot. An early warning signal like this needs to be analysed in conjunction with other factors which you normally take into account when making your investment decisions.

Watching the trend is not the only way to use relative strength. I particularly like to use it to *confirm* actual price movements. A move in a share price accompanied by a similar move by the relative strength is likely to be more reliable than one which is not. For instance, if a price breaks upwards out of a rectangle accompanied by an improvement in relative strength, it is a much stronger 'buy' signal than it would be without such accompaniment. The technical – or charting – term for this is **Confirmation** and is shown below in *Figure 30*. The jargon of the marketplace is of the relative strength 'confirming', or 'not confirming', a move.

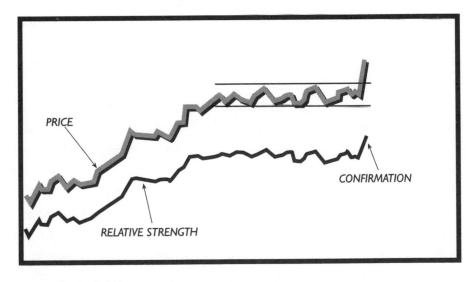

Figure 30: Confirmation.

If you see a price breaking out of a chart pattern, check the relative strength before you act. It will cut down your margin of error. The price plot and relative strength curve combined become a powerful duo.

Rate of Change Indicator (R.O.C.), or R.S.I.

This handy indicator is mainly used to identify *short-term* tops and bottoms in prices. Its inventor is an American, J Welles Wilder Jr., who has a penchant for mathematical equations. He called this indicator the 'Relative Strength Index', or R.S.I., but as we at Investment Research of Cambridge were already extensively using a relative strength indicator, as just described, we re-named the R.S.I.

We called it the Rate of Change Indicator, or R.O.C. The initial results we got from it were stunning; so much so that it became incorporated in one of our regular chart publications which deals with short-term movements for share traders.

I've seen the R.O.C. used in many ways but I will confine myself to the way I use it and then leave you to experiment with it. As I have said, this is a short-term indicator. It is generally calculated over a 14 day price history although it is a matter of finding out what period suits your own needs.

What it does is to measure the momentum, or velocity, of the movement of a price, hence our name Rate of Change Indicator. It lets you know when the price has moved too fast for its own good and that a better opportunity awaits those who are prepared to hold off.

The complicated formula is contained in Appendix Two on page 153 and you will ideally want a computer to calculate it. The resulting figure ranges between 0 and 100 (mathematically it is impossible for it to go outside this range). The 50 level is considered to be the 'neutral' figure. But it is extremes of movement which have the most significance.

In most instances the 70 level is considered 'overbought' and the 30 level denotes 'oversold'. But here a word of caution: some shares have proved to be more volatile than the norm and the R.O.C. has sometimes lead me astray; the 80 and 20 levels have proved to be the significant limits in some cases. So be careful and get to understand the nature and volatility of the shares you want to follow. Learn the characteristics of each.

So how do you deal with the R.O.C. in practice? If we take the example of Shell in 1994 and plot the daily range and close on arithmetic paper we can add the R.O.C. below the price chart. You will see in *Figure 31* on the next page that the R.O.C. appears to be quite volatile and this is normally the case This is because it is calculated over just 14 working days of price changes – less than three weeks in all. If it is going to operate satisfactorily the R.O.C. should be able to pick out the peaks and troughs in price.

In *Figure 31* see how the peaks and troughs in price are picked out by the peaks and troughs in the R.O.C. As it dips towards 30 or rises near 70, the price reverses its path.

This is the R.O.C. in its simplest usage. Indeed it is the only way I personally use it. But there is a school of thought, begun by Welles Wilder in his papers, which suggests that it can also be used as a confirmatory indicator in a similar way to the relative strength curve described earlier in this chapter. For instance, the new high in the share price during the late Summer of 1994 was not accompanied by a similar move in the R.O.C. and this was, perhaps, a warning that the price rise was becoming overdone. The price was rising too fast, too soon.

However, I am not convinced that this works well enough to be useful. In my experience there are far too many occasions where there has been such confirmation and yet the price has still failed to behave as expected.

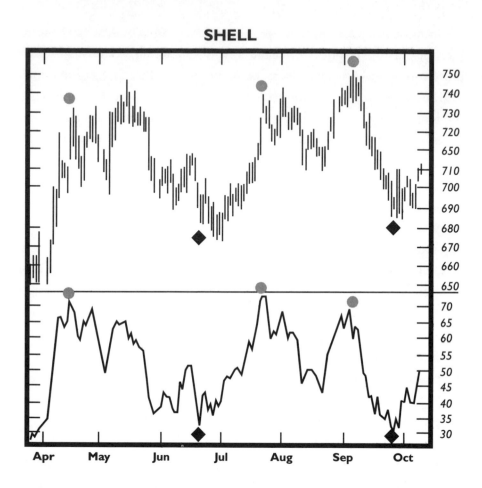

Figure 31: R.O.C.: Peaks and Troughs.

I have spent many hours studying this phenomenon and have come to the conclusion that in too many cases the R.O.C. is mathematically too high or too low to be able to physically continue in the same direction. If Shell *Figure 31* above has peaked once at, say, 750p with the R.O.C. at over 70 and the price then falls away, it is hardly a great idea to wait until the price moves into new high ground at, say, 760p accompanied by the R.O.C. at a higher level. The very high level of the R.O.C. at this point argues against you buying, so the fact that you have confirmation of the price move from the absolute level of the R.O.C. is of little consequence. All it is going to do is become even more overbought!

So I use it as a 'don't do' indicator. When it is high it tells me not to follow the crowd into the market and when it is low it stops me selling shares at too low a price. I always say that it stops me throwing myself out of a ground floor window!

Again I would stress that this is a personal view. There are many people using charts who seem to be able to come to terms with this but I cannot rationalise it in my own mind and it has let me down too many times for me to justify any great faith in it. But I do find the R.O.C. invaluable as a warning not to follow the crowd at the wrong moment.

Moving Averages

Most of us understand what an average is. But I have seen my seminar audiences shrink with fear at the concept of *moving* averages. It's very simple really.

An average is calculated by adding up a series of prices and dividing the result of that sum by the number of prices involved. A moving average is a similar calculation but the numbers making up the calculation change each day. Take, for instance, the price series for the FT-SE 100 Index in the first eleven trading days of October 1994:-

Monday 3rd	2983.5
Tuesday 4th	3001.8
Wednesday 5th	2956.3
Thursday 6th	2984.4
Friday 7th	2998.7

Monday 10th	3032.3
Tuesday 11th	3073.0
Wednesday 12th	3100.5
Thursday 13th	3141.9
Friday 14th	3106.7
Monday 17th	3120.2

If you add up the closing prices for the first ten trading days (October 3rd - 14th) you get a total of 30379.1. If you divide this by 10 you will get a result 3037.91. This is the 10 day average. To calculate the 10 day average for the period covering days 2-11, you omit the price for day 1 (October 3rd) from the calculation and substitute the price for day 11 (October 17th) :-

2983.5	
3001.8	3001.8
2956.3	2956.3
2984.4	2984.4
2998.7	2998.7
3032.3	3032.3
3073.0	3073.0
3100.5	3100.5
3141.9	3141.9
3106.7	3106.7
30379.1	3120.2
÷ 10 = 3037.91	30515.8
	÷ 10 = 3051.58

If you repeat this exercise daily you will be calculating a 10 day average on a rolling basis – the 'moving' average. I have used 10 days here for the sake of convenience and simplicity but analysts use all sorts of periods, depending on what they want to know. The most common series are 10, 20, 50, 100 and 200 days.

A 200 day moving average, for instance, covers a sufficiently long period to iron out any short-term bumps and troughs. It will represent a sort of trendline which will indicate the main direction of the market. In a

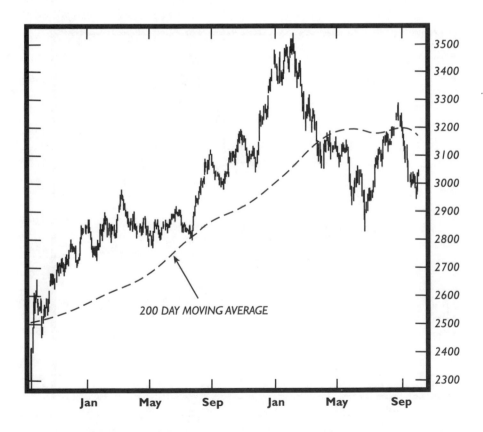

Figure 32: FT-SE 100 Index 200 day moving average. (1993–1994).

rising trend it will be below the price curve because, by definition, most of the prices which are included in the calculation will be lower than the latest price. In a falling market the majority of the prices will be above the present price and the moving average will be above the price curve. If we superimpose a 200 day moving average on a chart it will look like *Figure 32* .

However, if you need to make short-term investment decisions, a 200 day moving average is going to prove inadequate and you will have to use a shorter one. A 10 day moving average might be too sensitive; perhaps a 20

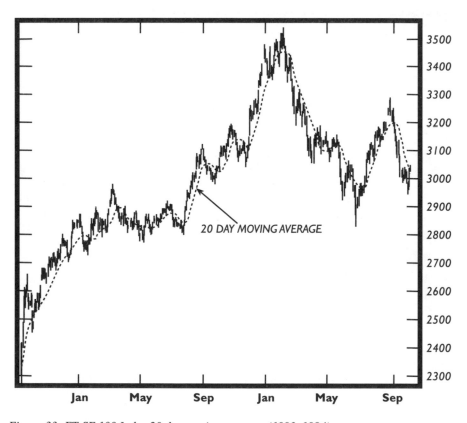

Figure 33: FT-SE 100 Index 20 day moving average. (1993–1994).

day calculation would be more appropriate. *Figure 33* on page 66 shows this on the same price chart. You will see immediately that it is less smooth than the 200 day moving average. This is because, being taken over a shorter time period a few spiky price movements have a more dramatic effect.

Whatever time periods are appropriate for your needs, one moving average on its own is going to be of little use to you. You need to keep two together and observe the interaction between them. Then they start to become useful and give you messages which can alert you to changes in the market. The points where the two moving averages cross over each other will become important parts of your strategy and tactics. But there are some important rules for you to remember.

The crossing over of two moving averages is a mathematical certainty from time to time. There is nothing remarkable about it. If a price begins to slow down, or even go into reverse, after an active period, the moving average covering the shorter of the two timescales will begin to change first. Being made up of a shorter series of prices it is more volatile than a moving average which is calculated from a larger number of prices.

Where these crossovers do become significant is when they happen with both moving averages moving in the same direction as each other.

This phenomenon often occurs at significant points on the chart and should alert you to the possibility that a potentially very profitable, or even damaging, move is in prospect. Let's have a look at another example, using the FT-SE 100 Index with a 20 day and a 50 day moving average and concentrate on the crossover in September 1992 in *Figure 34* which follows on page 68.

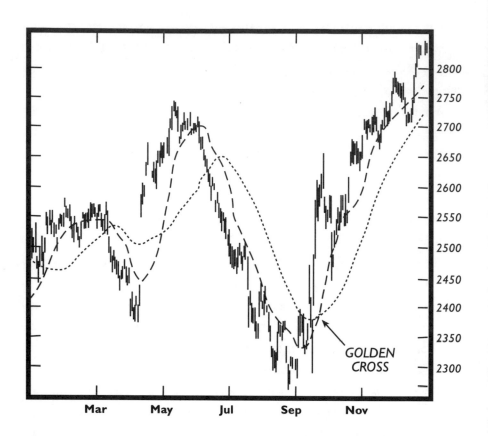

Figure 34: FT-SE 100 Index: Golden Cross.

In this case the moving averages were both rising when the crossover occurred; this gave a bullish signal. In technical terms this is called a Golden Cross. It is really quite reliable, although of course not infallible. It alerts you to a potential opportunity and will lead you to examine some of the other indicators I have already described and, of course, the price pattern itself. The latter may seem an obvious point but you would be surprised at how many technicians get carried away by the crossover's message and then forget the basics!

If the moving averages are both falling when they cross over each other the message is a bearish one. A movement like this is known as a 'dead cross' and it alerts you to a situation which is deteriorating. It is a warning signal that all is not well and if the price pattern has already begun to worry you, this may be the confirmation which finally makes you decide to sell. The most recent example of this, at the time of writing, is late September 1994 when the FT-SE 100 Index gave a clear bearish signal (*Figure 35 below*).

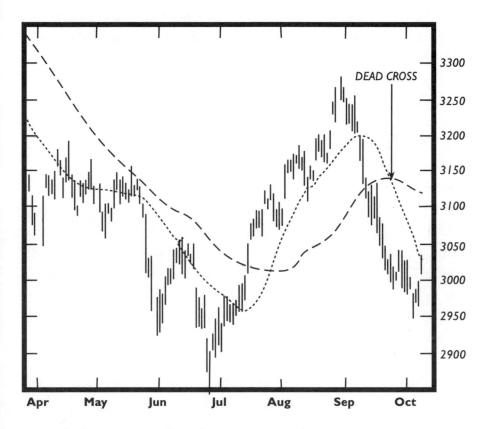

Figure 35: FT-SE 100 Index: Dead Cross.

As with many indicators, moving averages are not infallible. I prefer to use them in conjunction with other factors, such as the patterns which have been examined earlier, or the volume of trading in the shares at the time.

Volume

You will remember from Chapter Two that volume is normally plotted in vertical bar format at the bottom of the chart. I explained that if it was plotted in linear format the chart would become very cluttered and unappealing to the eye and, consequently, more difficult to use.

Plotting the volume every day can be a boring task if you keep your charts manually because it will tell you very little in normal day-to-day trading. Each day it is a little bit higher or lower than the day before but it goes up and down in a most uninteresting fashion.

However, once every few months, or even years, it can shout at you to do something at very critical points in the market cycle. Volume tends to go mad at market tops and bottoms, although in rather different ways.

Market tops tend to occur when volume has been building up steadily over a period of time. The market has been rising strongly and public interest growing. I well remember the period before the 1987 'Crash'. The stock-market was being discussed at dinner parties. Even people who had no money were becoming interested in borrowing some in order to buy shares because of others' stories of big profits on Mrs. Thatcher's privatisation issues.

The result was an increase in business in the market as people put their words into deeds. This led, as we now know, to an unhealthy explosion in share prices which became unsustainable. In the first 6 months of 1987 the FT-SE 100 Index rose by some 40%. The volume built up like a volcano getting ready to blow and sure enough the market eventually had a fall as shown in *Figure 36* on the next page.

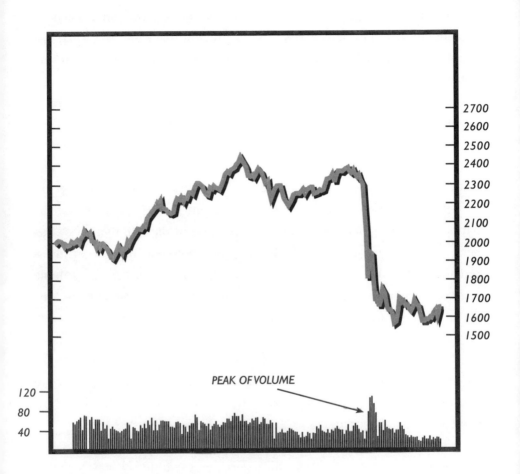

PEAK OF VOLUME

Figure 36: FT-SE 100 Index – 1987.

Volume in bear markets tends to behave rather differently. Falling prices are a complete turn-off for most investors and business in the market tends to shrink away as indifference accumulates. Only when prices begin to accelerate downwards, causing many investors to lose their nerve, does volume begin to increase. Eventually, when all the news is awful, the number of sellers retreating from the market begins to grow and this ends in a panic. Look at the chart of 1987 on the previous page and see where the average investor pulled out. Sadly, it's not difficult to spot, even for an untrained eye.

Frequently the end of a long bear market happens when a major company goes bust, causing much of the loss of nerve I have described. In 1969 it was the demise of Vehicle & General Insurance and Rolls Royce; in 1973/4 it was Burmah Oil. It seems amazing now, incidentally, to think that two of these have been resurrected and are quoted on the market again.

1987 was different. No large company went spectacularly bust at the bottom of the fall. Because of the short duration of the fall, there has even been academic debate as to whether it was a real bear market, or just a setback within the context of a long bull market. Nevertheless, volume reached an enormous spike as private investors lost their nerve in a big way. Awful reports on the television news and in the press had become unbearably depressing and pushed them over the edge.

The huge volume of dealings told you that the bear phase could be over. Of course you could not take this one signal in isolation and there was little else to encourage you to buy at the time. But it was one of the first signs that things could be changing.

Incidentally, there is a school of thought that volume nowadays is less significant than before. Big fund managers don't tend to sell any longer if they are worried about the market; the Futures and Traded Options markets provide them with the means of hedging their positions. And the private investor now accounts for a much smaller proportion of the dealings in direct shares, having turned to unit trusts for safety and more variety.

I don't buy this argument as far as private investors are concerned. They still sell their unit trusts if they think they are going to lose their money and in turn the unit trust manager has to sell something to cover the withdrawal of cash from his fund. It may be, of course that we should now be keeping charts of unit trust sales and purchases. The figures are published every month and are freely available, so why not?

In fact this is already being done. Time will tell whether it is going to be a useful exercise but certainly in the US it has been a very helpful pointer at times.

I conclude that volume should be regarded as another tool in your box of indicators. Just as in the case of your tool box in your workshop at home, you won't need all the contents all of the time. But they're there when you need them. And if you haven't got the right tool for the job then you are unlikely to do it well.

Meisels' Indicator

In 1980 I attended a conference held by the then embryonic US Market Technicians Association in Chatham, Cape Cod, Massachusetts. There were many speakers who had done pioneering work and I was overawed by the amount of information which was available to investors. Everything from housing starts to mutual fund (unit trust) sales figures every month. The experts there were all professional fund managers and stockbrokers who were trying to find early warning signals in the markets.

One speaker was particularly fascinating. Ron Meisels, a broker from across the border in Canada, had done a lot of work on a very simple indicator which dealt with the short-term outlook for the market index, in this case the Dow Jones Industrial Average. The calculation was simplicity itself – always an attraction for a non-mathematician like me – and could be worked out on the back of an envelope. But what struck me about it was its long track record. Ron showed the indicator in action since 1895 and it was quite uncanny how well it worked.

The calculation is made over a 10 day period, based on the closing price of the index each day. For each day the index closes higher, a score of +1 is registered while for each day the market closes lower, the score is -1. On the rare days the market is unchanged, a 0 is put into the calculation.

So let's imagine that in the last 10 days the market has closed better on 6 occasions and down on 4. It does not take mathematical genius to calculate that the result will be +2. If there are 8 days when the market has fallen and only 2 where it has risen, the indicator will be -6. And so on.

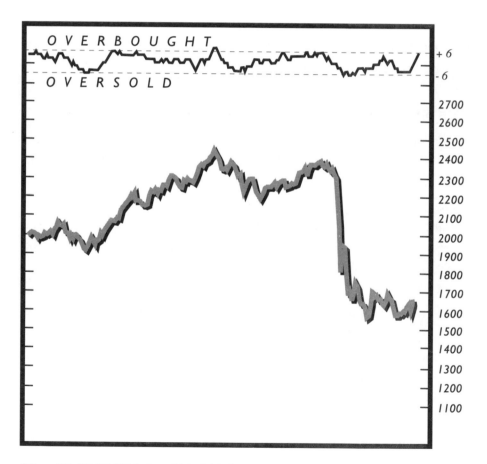

Figure 37: FT-SE 100 Index – Meisels' Indicator.

When the indicator is plotted onto chart paper, peaks and troughs will appear like *Figure 37* on page 74.

Ron Meisels argued that the market was becoming overbought (too high in the short-term) or oversold (too low) when the indicator hit the +6 or -6 levels. At these points it would be wrong to chase after prices and it would pay you to hold off until the indicator returned towards neutral (0) before activating your order. And it's as simple as that.

I have been using the indicator for analysing major market indices for 14 years and while it does have some limitations – and at times, irritations – it is very useful indeed when used in conjunction with, say, the Rate of Change. If you are a long-term investor, then it's probably not worth the effort as it is a very short-term tool but if market timing is important to you then time spent on the Meisels' will probably be well used.

Conclusion: By using a combination of the auxilliary indicators covered in this chapter you should be able to read your charts with greater success. Use them all and find out over a period of time which ones suit you best. It will take patience and time but eventually you will get to the point where you will be one step ahead of the rest.

If you are a shorter term investor/trader you will have *not* only a way of deciding when to take profits or losses but also an indication of when not to do something – just knowing when to sit on your hands can save you a lot of money.

SIX

OTHER INDICATORS

Although I have concentrated on stocks and shares so far, charts are widely used in other markets. Many commodity and currency dealers and traders would not dream of being without them, for instance. You yourself do not need to confine yourself to watching share prices on their own. Indeed I would strongly advise that you do not.

Interest rates, for example, exert a strong influence upon all capital markets. Rising long-term rates, especially, will tend to depress share prices, for instance, while falling rates are usually at the backbone of a bull market.

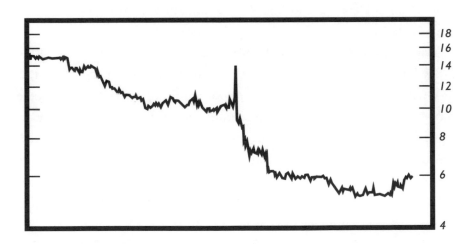

Figure 38: Interest rate chart: 3 Months Interbank Rate (1986–1994).

So it pays to know what is likely to happen to them next. Economists are unlikely to be much help to you at critical turning points but the markets, and hence the charts, react quickly to changing circumstances. Try keeping the 3 months Interbank rate on log paper. You'll be surprised at the results over an economic cycle. I have shown it in *Figure 38* on page 77. It covers the period from 1986 to 1994. The blip in the middle is an event you probably remember – the UK's exit from the ERM.

I always believe that it pays to be an independent thinker and not follow the crowd. Admittedly it is difficult when you read a daily newspaper or listen to the news but if you can train yourself to take a jaundiced view of what is being reported you will gradually get ahead of the game.

Other generally available information can be helpful at times. As discussed earlier, statistics are published on unit trust sales and repurchases, for instance, and may give you a good indication of what the private investor is doing. Sales tend to reach a high as the market itself reaches its high and the bulk of repurchases tend to come near market low points as disillusioned investors unload their poorly timed purchases with the economy at its blackest. The theory is that the little man is always wrong but you don't have to be.

You can also divide the yield on gilt-edged stocks by the yield on the FT-SE 100 Index and plot the result on arithmetic scale paper. I do this every day so that I am aware at the important times when shares become overvalued (especially) or undervalued compared with fixed interest stocks.

For example, study *Figure 39* on page 79 and notice the peak which formed in 1987, ahead of the Crash. It meant that equities were becoming overvalued. The norm on this calculation is somewhere between 1.9 and 2.2, so any movement outside these parameters attracts my attention and forces me to re-examine my reasons for my strategy.

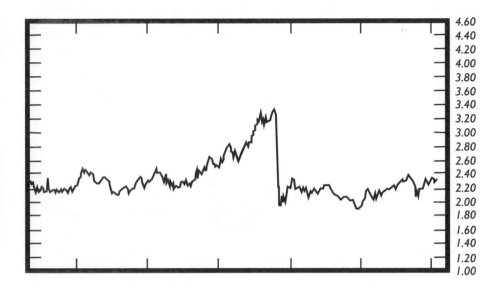

Figure 39: The Yield Gap Ratio. (1984–1990).

The chart may be useful only once in an economic cycle but when it speaks to you it is usually very important to your financial health.

If you are occasionally attracted to gold shares, try plotting the ratio of the F.T. Gold Mines Index to the price of the metal itself. The resulting chart will show you how relatively overvalued or undervalued the general run of shares are when compared to the gold price. On occasions you will get some important messages as the shares tend to be much more sensitive than the metal. This is because the companies' mining costs are constant and the fluctuations in the metal price have a big influence on mining company profits.

Figure 40 on page 80 shows the ratio of gold shares to the price of gold for the period from 1984 to 1988.

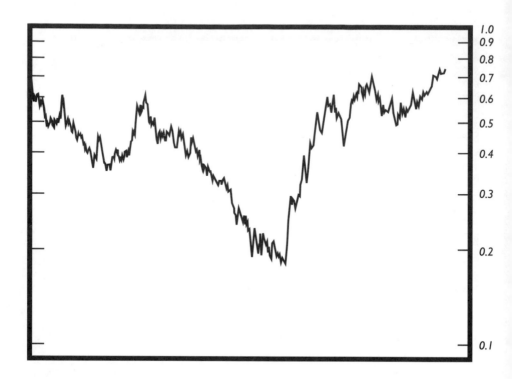

Figure 40: Gold shares/gold price ratio. (1984–1988).

The list of what is possible goes on and on. But don't always expect ratio charts to conform to the patterns described earlier. The *absolute* levels of the charts of these calculations are more likely to be significant, rather than the shapes which evolve. As I have noted, many such charts only give you a signal infrequently but they can save you a lot of mistakes.

Consider the sort of things **you** have always thought have a great influence on prices. Keep some charts of them over a period of time and see if you can discover something useful. Even dividing the market index by another market index may allow you to see familiar support and resistance points building up, which could well help you with the timing of switches, if you are an active investor. Half the fun is in using your imagination and trying to get one step ahead of the rest.

SEVEN

PUTTING THEORY INTO PRACTICE

So now you should be well on your way to becoming an expert in the use of charts in your decision making process. However, there is still the most common problem I find facing the private investor. How do you find the information to start keeping your own charts? And even if you go to the expense of buying a computer and the software to go with it, does Ceefax or some similar electronic source have all the information you're going to need?

Your needs are going to be particular to you, of course. No two investors are likely to want to keep an eye on precisely the same charts. And what you follow day-to-day will change from time to time, depending on developments in the markets and how adventurous you want to be with your investment strategy.

For most investors, the *Financial Times* is a rich source of information if you know where to look and what to do with it once you've found it. A daily 65p is probably as cheap as the bus fare to the local library to read it free of charge, so grit your teeth and order it from your newsagent. There's nothing more frustrating than going into the shop following an active day in the markets, only to find that the few copies they stock have been sold. Incidentally, don't bother with the Monday issue. For chartists there is no additional information contained in it, following the market reports in Saturday's edition.

Decide upon some key economic indicators you want to watch. They don't have to be complicated but they will give you a developing background to the equity (or share) market which you will be primarily interested in. Perhaps I could make some suggestions to get you started.

Interest rates influence most financial markets. They divide into short-term, which reflect the immediate prospects for the economy, to long-term ones which are a general indication of confidence in the future. The latter are best represented by gilt-edged stock prices, or yields. When long-term yields rise and prices fall, the City and other investors are becoming wary of inflationary prospects (these worries may or may not be well-founded but nevertheless they do affect sentiment, which is a prime mover of share prices).

UK INTEREST RATES

LONDON MONEY RATES

Mar 29	Over-night	7 days notice	One month	Three months	Six months	One year
Interbank Sterling	$6\frac{7}{8}$ - $5\frac{1}{4}$	$6\frac{7}{16}$ - $6\frac{3}{16}$	$6\frac{7}{16}$ - $6\frac{1}{4}$	$6\frac{3}{4}$ - $6\frac{9}{16}$	$7\frac{1}{8}$ - 7	$7\frac{11}{16}$ - $7\frac{9}{16}$
Sterling CDs	-	-	$6\frac{11}{32}$ - $6\frac{7}{32}$	$6\frac{5}{8}$ - $6\frac{9}{16}$	$7\frac{1}{16}$ - $6\frac{15}{16}$	$7\frac{9}{16}$ - $7\frac{7}{16}$
Treasury Bills	-	-	$6\frac{1}{8}$ - $6\frac{1}{16}$	$6\frac{5}{16}$ - $6\frac{1}{4}$	-	-
Bank Bills	-	-	$6\frac{1}{8}$ - $6\frac{1}{16}$	$6\frac{13}{32}$ - $6\frac{11}{32}$	$6\frac{13}{16}$ - $6\frac{3}{4}$	-
Local authority deps.	$6\frac{5}{16}$ - $6\frac{3}{16}$	$6\frac{5}{16}$ - $6\frac{3}{16}$	$6\frac{5}{16}$ - $6\frac{3}{16}$	$6\frac{5}{8}$ - $6\frac{1}{2}$	$7\frac{1}{16}$ - $6\frac{15}{16}$	$7\frac{9}{16}$ - $7\frac{7}{16}$
Discount Market deps	$6\frac{3}{4}$ - $5\frac{1}{4}$	$6\frac{3}{8}$ - $6\frac{1}{8}$	-	-	-	-

3 Months Interbank Rate

Figure 41: FT: interest rates.

Look in the FT, about ten or eleven pages from the back of the prices section and you will find tables which appear every day. They contain vital information you need. The first *Figure 41* above is a table of short-term interest rates of different kinds. I use the 3 months Interbank rate because it's quite sensitive to developments in the short-term economic picture - not too long a period and not too short. In simple terms this is the rate of interest used between the banks and it is a good indication of the immediate temperature of short-term interest rates as a whole. Take the two figures quoted and take the average of the two.

FT-ACTUARIES FIXED INTEREST INDICES

Price Indices UK Gilts	Wed Mar 29	Day's change %	Tue Mar 28	Accrued interest	xd adj. ytd
1 Up to 5 years (24)	119.32	−0.19	119.54	1.65	2.89
2 5-15 years (21)	140.12	−0.43	140.72	2.12	3.18
3 Over 15 years (9)	156.12	−0.51	156.92	1.65	4.05
4 Irredeemables (6)	179.83	−0.79	181.27	3.31	1.47
5 All stocks (60)	136.97	−0.36	137.47	1.91	3.22
Index-linked					
6 Up to 5 years (2)	190.01	−0.03	190.08	−0.06	2.57
7 Over 5 years (11)	175.15	0.34	175.74	0.76	1.2
8 All stocks (13)	175.78	−0.31	176.32	0.68	1

Average gross redemption yields are shown above. Coupon Bands: Low: 0%-7¾%; Medium

Over 15 Years Stock Index

Figure 42: FT: Government stocks.

Nearby you will find the table of gilt-edged information from the previous day: *Figure 42* above. Gilts, or Government stocks, are a bellweather of longer term confidence. Use an index rather than the price of an individual stock where the approach of the redemption date will influence the price. I prefer the Over 15 Years Stocks Index rather than the All Stocks Index which includes short life stocks. A chart of the Over 15 Years Stocks will give you an idea of what is going on in the all-important long-term interest rate markets. These are valuable indications to the equity market.

The FT-SE 100 Share Index is the most popularly followed of all the share indices because it's updated continuously throughout the trading

FT - SE Actuaries Share Indices — The UK Series

	Mar 29	Day's chge%	Mar 28	Mar 27	Mar 24	Year ago	Div. yield%	Earn. yield%	P/E ratio	Xd adj. ytd	Total Return
FT-SE 100	3142.3	+0.4	3128.3	3149.8	3153.4	3092.4	4.35	7.88	15.34	44.44	1217.13
FT-SE Mid 250	3421.8	+0.2	3416.2	3419.9	3419.7	3767.1	3.75	6.76	17.89	25.75	1299.01
FT-SE Mid 250 ex Inv Trusts	3430.0	+0.2	3423.3	3427.1	3427.4	3787.8	3.90	7.32	16.64	25.86	1300.28
FT-SE-A 350	1558.7	+0.4	1552.8	1561.4	1562.8	1574.1	4.21	7.63	15.85	19.75	1233.59
FT-SE-A 350 Higher Yield	1571.0	+0.4	1564.3	1573.1	1577.7	1579.4	5.18	8.45	14.22	26.98	1026.30
FT-SE-A 350 Lower Yield	1546.5	+0.3	1541.3	1549.9	1547.5	1528.2	3.08	6.67	18.29	12.13	1027.64
FT-SE SmallCap	1709.34	......	1709.20	1708.22	1704.63	1921.93	3.54	5.34	23.34	13.04	1346.33
FT-SE SmallCap ex Inv Trusts	1686.41	+0.1	1685.47	1684.81	1682.40	1898.30	3.76	5.97	21.12	12.78	1332.68
FT-SE-A ALL-SHARE	1538.43	+0.4	1533.00	1540.81	1541.81	1566.15	4.16	7.45	16.25	18.90	1237.68

■ FT-SE Actuaries All-Share

	Mar 29	Day's	Mar 28	Mar 27	Mar 24	Year ago	Div. yield%	Earn yield%	P/E ratio	Xd adj. ytd	Total Return
[illegible]INERAL EXTRA[illegible](24)	2696[illegible]		[illegible].10	2683.63	2702.8[illegible]		3.81	6.6[illegible]	9.00	50.5[illegible]	[illegible]109.42
[illegible]	3[illegible]			[illegible]			3.91		[illegible]25	9[illegible]	[illegible]7.23
[illegible]		+0.3	190[illegible]			[illegible]1939.23			13[illegible]		
79 Property(4[illegible]	[illegible]11	+0.4	1369.11	13[illegible]	[illegible]70.85	1571.32	[illegible]	[illegible]30	23.72	4.58	
80 INVESTMENT [illegible]RUSTS(133)	26[illegible]0.99	−0.2	2616.83	2619.87	2614.01	2811.07	2.44	1.98	50.59	18.32	18.90
89 FT-SE-A ALL-SHARE(915)	1538.43	+0.4	1533.00	1540.81	1541.81	1566.15	4.16	7.45	16.25	18.90	1237.68
FT-SE-A Fledgling	955.59	−0.1	956.24	956.41	954.21	–	3.09	–	–	6.54	962.05
FT-SE-A Fledgling ex Inv Trusts	952.73	−0.1	953.35	953.63	951.87	–	3.27	–	–	6.70	959.33

■ Hourly movements

	Open	9.00	10.00	11.00	12.00	13.00	14.00	15.00	16.10	High/day	Low/day
FT-SE 100	3125.3	3112.7	3116.7	3120.3	3129.7	3127.0	3126.7	3128.3	3140.4	3142.3	3111.3
FT-SE Mid 250	3414.3	3412.4	3412.0	3412.8	3415.7	3418.0	3418.4	3418.4	3421.2	3421.8	3411.0
FT-SE-A 350	1551.4	1546.4	1547.9	1549.3	1553.2	1552.4	1552.4	1553.0	1558.0	1558.7	1545.7

Time of FT-SE 100 Day's high: 4.28pm Day's low: 9.21am. FT-SE 100 1994 High: 3520.3(2/2/94) Low: 2876.6(24/6/94) .

Figure 43: FT-SE Actuaries share indices.

hours of the Stock Exchange. Its progress is reported in several places in the FT but the most comprehensive information is contained in the FT-SE Actuaries Share Indices table: *Figure 43* above. Here you can get not only the close for the previous day but also the highest and lowest level of the day so that you can keep a daily range and close chart (see Chapter Two). I've circled the two places where the information is contained.

You will see that this table also contains all the information on the sector indices for the market as well as the indices for smaller shares and so on. There is a wealth of information here but unless you are a larger investor with a big portfolio it probably isn't worth keeping much of this in chart form. But cut the table out of the paper each day and paste it in a scrapbook for future reference; one day you might need it for a special project. The table also gives you the price/earnings ratio and yield for the broad stockmarket, in the form of the All-Share Index, which I have marked with squares. These can be worth plotting if you have time; sometimes they can give early warnings of change in the market background.

The formerly popular FT 30 Share - or 'Ordinary' - Index is quoted in a separate table and is probably not worth plotting. But the table contains a further piece of valuable information which you should plot on your FT-SE 100 chart - the day's volume – *Figure 44* below. This can be recorded in the form of the number of share trades done, or their total value. As the latter are computed and reported a full day later than the number of trades I prefer up to date information and plot the number of trades.

FINANCIAL TIMES EQUITY INDICES

	Mar 29	Mar 28	Mar 27	Mar 24	Mar 23	Yr ago	*High	*Low
Ordinary Share	2405.9	2395.4	2417.4	2413.0	2398.7	2445.5	**2713.6**	2238.3
Ord. div. yield	4.39	4.42	4.38	4.39	4.42	3.80	**4.66**	3.43
Earn. yld. % full	7.15	7.19	7.12	7.15	7.19	5.19	**7.39**	3.82
P/E ratio net	16.66	16.57	16.72	16.67	16.56	20.94	**33.43**	16.11
P/E ratio nil	16.48	16.39	16.54	16.49	16.38	21.82	**30.80**	15.77

*For 1994/5, Ordinary Share index since compilation: high 2713.6 2/02/94; low 49.4 26/6/40
FT Ordinary Share index base date 1/7/35.

Ordinary Share hourly changes

Open	9.00	10.00	11.00	12.00	13.00	14.00	15.00	16.00	High	Low
2393.5	2385.1	2386.1	2389.1	2394.8	2392.2	2391.8	2392.4	2400.1	2405.9	2383.3

	Mar 29	Mar 28	Mar 27	Mar 24	Mar 23	Yr ago
SEAQ bargains	34,820	35,707	33,734	29,083	34,541	46,348
Equity turnover (£m)†	–	1443.7	1411.9	1703.3	1766.6	1759.2
Equity bargains†	–	45,664	47,334	41,775	47,054	55,855
Shares traded (ml)†	–	682.2	653.4	727.5	777.1	674.1

†Excluding intra-market business and overseas turnover.

Figure 44: SEAQ bargains.

In *Figure 39* on page 79 I showed the use of the yield gap ratio. To calculate this I use the yield on Consolidated Stock, or Consols, $2^1/2\%$ and the yield on the FT-SE 100. Consols is a reasonable guide to gilt-edged stock yields and because the stock is irredeemable its history goes back many years and there is no redemption date to influence the price. The yield on Consols is in the gilt-edged stocks table and the yield on the FT-SE 100 is quoted in the FT-Actuaries Indices table shown in *Figure 45* below. Divide the Consols yield by the FT-SE 100 yield each day to obtain the Yield Gap Ratio and keep your eye on it. Chapter 6 deals with this indicator.

FT - SE Actuaries Share Indices										The UK Series	
	Day's Mar 29	chge%	Mar 28	Mar 27	Mar 24	Year ago	Div. yield%	Earn. yield%	P/E ratio	Xd adj. ytd	Total Return
FT-SE 100	3142.3	+0.4	3128.3	3149.8	3153.4	3092.4	4.35	7.88	15.34	44.44	1217.13
FT-SE Mid 250	3421.8	+0.2	3416.2	3419.9	3419.7	3767.1	3.75	6.76	17.89	25.75	1299.01
FT-SE Mid 250 ex Inv Trusts	3430.0	+0.2	3423.3	3427.1	3427.4	3787.8	3.90	7.32	16.64	25.86	1300.28
FT-SE-A 350	1558.7	+0.4	1552.8	1561.4	1562.8	1574.1	4.21	7.63	15.85	19.75	1233.59
FT-SE-A 350 Higher Yield	1571.0	+0.4	1564.3	1573.1	1577.7	1579.4	5.18	8.45	14.22	26.98	1026.30
FT-SE-A 350 Lower Yield	1546.5	+0.3	1541.3	1549.9	1547.5	1528.2	3.08	6.67	18.29	12.13	1027.64
FT-SE SmallCap	1709.34	......	1709.20	1708.22	1704.63	1921.93	3.54	5.34	23.34	13.04	1346.33
FT-SE SmallCap ex Inv Trusts	1686.41	+0.1	1685.47	1684.81	1682.40	1898.30	3.76	5.97	21.12	12.78	1332.66
FT-SE-A ALL-SHARE	1538.43	+0.4	1533.00	1540.81	1541.81	1566.15	4.16	7.45	16.25	18.90	1237.68

■ FT-SE Actuaries All-Share											
	Day's Mar 29		Mar 28	Mar 27	Mar 24	Year ago	Div. yield%	Earn. yield%	P/E ratio	Xd adj. ytd	Total Return
MINERAL EXTRAC... I(24)	2696		..10	2683.63	2702.8...		3.81	6.65	9.00	50.5...	109.42

Figure 45: FT-SE 100 Index yield.

Overseas markets - especially New York - can exert an important influence on London and a few larger ones such as Tokyo or Frankfurt should be watched too. If you are a larger investor you may well have diversified into one or two of these via unit trusts or investment trusts. Any enthusiasm or panics here can sometimes rub off on London. Americans I speak to claim that they watch London as it has already been open for a number of hours before Wall Street opens. But London market investors have always told me that when Wall Street sneezes, the rest of the world catches a cold. Certainly it is inescapable that the US economy and the level of US interest rates exert a big influence on the rest of us. So find the day's high/low/close for the Dow Jones Industrial Average and plot it together with the volume. I've circled all these to make it easy for you in *Figure 46* on page 89. The other overseas markets are on the same page,

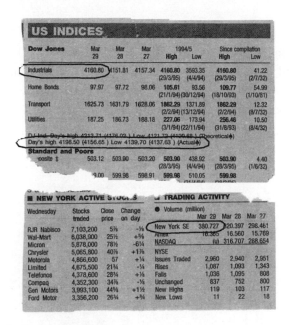

Figure 46: Dow Jones Industrial Average.

in the adjoining table. US interest rates, however are quoted on the very front page of the FT and the 3-months Treasury Bill Rate and the Long

Figure 47: US rates.

Bond yield will give you the short and long-term picture of interest rates: *Figure 47* on page 89.

The price of gold is on the Commodities and Agriculture page in this little table: *Figure 48*. Take the average of the two prices quoted for the close. If the market gets exciting, plot the 'morning fix' and 'afternoon fix' as the day's range too.

PRECIOUS METALS
■ **LONDON BULLION MARKET**
(Prices supplied by N M Rothschild)

Gold(Troy oz)	$ price	£ equiv	SFr equiv
Close	383.10-383.50		
Opening	382.80-383.20		
Morning fix	383.00	237.181	433.709
Afternoon fix	383.00	237.564	434.897
Day's High	383.90-384.30		
Day's Low	382.65-382.95		
Previous close	382.00-382.30		

Loco Ldn Mean Gold Lending Rates (Vs US$)

1 month 4.01	6 months 4.87
2 months 4.26	12 months 5.20
3 months 4.52	

Silver Fix	p/troy oz.	US cts equiv.
Spot	283.40	473.10
3 months	297.35	479.00
6 months	302.25	486.00
1 year	313.25	501.30

Gold Coins	$ price	£ equiv.
Krugerand	378-390	2^0-24

Figure 48: The gold price.

The broad brush of share prices is contained in the two large table pages at the back of the FT. It's just a matter of keeping what you are able to keep. A personal computer comes into its own here, of course.

Charts build up over a period of time and if you start with a blank grid it will be many months before you are getting any worthwhile patterns developing. Sadly, there are very few places these days where you can buy one-off copies of pre-plotted charts which you can then keep up to date. My company is one of them, however, and publishes an annual catalogue of what is available. They cost around £6.50 each including VAT and postage.

As a final courtesy to you, my patient reader, I am happy to offer

you five free charts, valued at more than twice the cost of this book, to get you off on the right track. Write to Investment Research of Cambridge Ltd, 28 Panton Street, Cambridge CB2 1DH, quoting the title of the book and they will be sent to you by return, absolutely free of charge, together with the latest catalogue. The charts I have selected are:

FT-SE 100 Share Index (Daily Range & Close) with volume

FT-SE Small Capitalisation Stocks Index

(keep your eye on the smaller companies)

3 Months Interbank rate

US 90 Day Bills

Dow Jones Industrial Average (Daily Range & Close) with volume

I regret that this list is not variable under this offer for economic reasons, as I'm sure you will appreciate.

Get started with these charts and see how you get on. At first you will find plotting them is slow and time consuming but once you become familiar with the scales you will get quicker and quicker, allowing more time for more charts. One final tip; plot with a sharp pencil to begin with, as you will make mistakes. Pencil plotting makes alterations easier to deal with.

As for your own individual investment strategy, I cannot advise you. It should, of course, fit your own risk profile and time horizons. But you will soon discover which charts and indicators are the most helpful to you and I am convinced that, given time, you will make better timing decisions on your investments than before. Don't forget to use your charts to determine your stop-loss levels when you buy; make use of the techniques I have described in this book.

Do read more books, especially any involving market timing and other indicators. I am sure it will be time well spent.

EIGHT

FINAL THOUGHTS

As I said in my introduction, this book should be regarded as a first step along a road of knowledge. I have deliberately omitted many other charting methods and indicators. You can further your knowledge by reading some of the more comprehensive books on the subject. Many are of American origin and are expensive and difficult to obtain. I have listed a few of the more easily available ones in the bibliography in Appendix One on page 151.

You can, if you wish, join The Society of Technical Analysts as an Associate Member which will entitle you to attend their monthly meetings and receive their journal 3 times a year. They also have a free and very comprehensive personal or postal lending library covering the subject in immense depth. Ultimately you may even want to take their exams and qualify for full membership (MSTA) although these are by no means compulsory. You can get in touch with the Membership Secretary at 28 Panton Street, Cambridge, Tel: 01223 356251, for details.

My own firm even runs regular two-day courses on the subject, to the Society's examination standards.

There are a number of good, cheap computer packages available which do all the calculations and plotting for you. Some systems can even update the prices and charts from Ceefax on your television. You don't have to sit down with a pencil and paper. Of course the computer doesn't take away the element of judgement and decision making away from you but it saves a lot of the drudgery of keeping the charts. We have used the 'Technical Analyst' package, available from Luton-based Synergy Software, Tel: 01582 424282 and have been impressed with its quality and flexibility. It contains most of the indicators I have described.

Indexia Research, based in Berkhamsted, Herts, Tel: 01442 878015 produces three levels of technical analysis packages and offers upgrades without penalty as you learn. It is a well-established company and the products are good.

Many more sophisticated systems are available, especially for the professional market; the cost is prohibitive for most private investors. They are normally on-line to the markets and among those we have seen are systems produced by Reuters, CQG, Knight Ridder, and ADP.

A one-stop source of information and advice is the Market Data Centre, 19/21 Great Tower Street, London EC3 5AQ, Tel: 0171 522 0094. They don't charge for their advice; they are paid by the product providers and can find a system to suit your needs which is compatible with your hardware.

On a personal level I still keep some charts by hand as I feel this adds an extra dimension to the 'feel' I get for prices. But then perhaps I am a little old-fashioned.

However you maintain them, charts will help to instill valuable disciplines into your investment strategy and you will learn to run profits or take them when appropriate. But more importantly you will recognise at a relatively early stage where, perhaps, an important change is occurring.

A target price which has been reached or a stop-loss level which has been triggered will at least make you sit down and re-examine why you are still holding the share. *Be prepared to change your mind if you think you're wrong; most sensible people do!*

But don't regard charts as the be-all-and-end-all of your investment problems. Use them in conjunction with your traditional methods of making decisions and over a period of time they should improve your timing and self-discipline.

As former US Vice-President, Dan Quayle, is reputed to have said:

"Predictions can be difficult, especially those involving the future ."

Good luck.

NINE

A DAY IN THE LIFE OF A TECHNICAL ANALYST

Perhaps the best way to show what chartists do is to describe how they spend their day. My own day is not really typical of the average chartist (if such an individual exists!) so what follows is a composite picture of a number of chartists I know. I will call him Peter.

7.00am

Peter's day starts pretty early. The firm he works for advises a number of clients in Europe and the Middle East on trends in everything from the price of oil and gold through to what's happening in UK shares. So with Continental markets open an hour before the UK, and Middle Eastern clients awake two hours before that, Peter is usually at his desk at around 7am.

Fortunately he only lives a short drive from the office so this is not too arduous. Peter also has the consolation that many of his City-based clients will already be at their desks having had hour-long train journeys!

Most chartists live or die by their 'feel' for the market. They need to be consistently right in their predictions better than six or seven times out of ten to retain the following they have painstakingly built up. Peter's firm is a small but long-established one, owned by its directors, with a number of lucrative consultancy clients. These range from City institutions, overseas clients, to companies and wealthy private individuals.

Peter gets his feel for the markets he follows by keeping a number of charts manually. Many chartists follow this discipline, which originated in the days before computers made generating charts much easier. Peter keeps about 100 charts of this type and spends the first half-hour or so of each day updating them by hand from the *Financial Times*. More often than not one of the 100 will be showing an interesting pattern which may call for further research and provide the basis for a money-making idea for the firm's clients.

The next task is to produce the daily sheet faxed to all the firm's clients giving an updated view on the market and selecting a share of the day. This is normally a stock that looks to be at a particular interesting point on its chart. Today the market happens to be trendless, but Peter is still able to highlight areas of support and resistance that the market indices may hit in due course.

Today's stock idea is Glaxo, whose share price chart caught Peter's eye the previous day. News in the morning paper regarding a US court ruling on a best-selling drug's patent life has provided the fundamental background to the earlier breakthrough a previous resistance point. Peter recommends buying the shares strongly on any pullback to the previous resistance level, since this should now constitute support.

10.30am

The morning is punctuated by colleagues walking into Peter's office to discuss different charts and the reaction of various world markets to the news of the day. One colleague, who manages funds on a discretionary basis for a number of clients, believes that the UK market has reached the end of its correction phase and is now likely to move up. He has been offered an attractive line of stock by a broker and wants to discuss the patterns shown up by the share price chart.

After some debate, the colleague decides to buy the stock and parcel it out among the different client portfolios. Like most chartists, though the charts take precedence, both Peter and his colleagues work on the basis of a mixture of technical indicators and the underlying fundamentals of particular stocks.

One example of this approach is Peter's weekly newsletter. Part of Peter's 'family' of research products, this looks mainly at UK companies. Each week's issue takes about a day to put together.

Once an attractive chart-based idea has been found, Peter spends some time checking out the fundamentals of the company, using the basic information sources available to most investors (*Hambro Company Guide, Estimate Directory,* and *McCarthy* press cuttings) to arrive at a composite picture. Writing is often done during the evening, when interruptions are fewer.

In a spare half-hour in the course of the morning, Peter takes time out to scroll through the basic technical indicators on a number of companies stored on his computer. The charts slowly rotate and Peter watches for a pattern that looks significant. "To be worth highlighting, the story has to leap out at you", he says. This process may be repeated two or three times in the course of a week, so that a subconscious knowledge is built up about the share price pattern of different companies and market indices.

When a particularly interesting pattern looks to have developed, Peter notes it down on his pad. At the end of this session, the particular resistance and break-out points for the share are programmed quickly into his 'Market-Eye' limit minder. The Market-Eye service from ICV is a real-time price display service. The limit minder can automatically monitor the level of all the prices stored on the system. This ensures that if any of the trend-lines or support levels on the charts Peter felt were particularly significant were to be broken, the screen would bleep and the appropriate share flash to draw attention to the move.

Lunchtime

Lunch is generally a sandwich at the desk or a quick bite in the pub across the road from the office. Peter's office is away from the hustle and bustle of the City, so there are comparatively few visits from clients in the course of a normal week.

This has its drawbacks. Clients up in the City often want Peter or one of his colleagues to attend late afternoon meetings to discuss the market and to hear his ideas. Today is one such day. Although the secretarial staff in the office have done a lot of work preparing charts and slides for the presentation, Peter takes the opportunity of the lunchtime lull to review what he is going to say about the market.

Many City types are still hostile to the idea of using charts for making investment decisions, so Peter often has to face a few sceptical questioners in his audience. The ideas he puts forward have to be strong enough to stand up to these challenges, so now, and on the train up to the City, Peter pores over the papers and rehearses his lines.

2.30pm

As Peter is about to leave for the station, one of his colleagues, the firm's compliance officer, charged with ensuring that the small firm fulfils all its regulatory obligations, reminds him that a form he was supposed to fill in a few days ago needs to be completed. Muttering about the endless form-filling on subjects ranging from the wording of advertisements, to staff dealing, how to handle new clients, and all the other regulatory tasks, Peter scrawls the necessary information in the appropriate boxes, signs the form and then, regulatory duty done, hurries off for his train.

The client meeting has in fact taken precedence over another regular task Peter has to undertake. Each month all the firm's directors sit down together and review their overall strategy and express views on the direction of the world's financial markets, currencies and commodities. The afternoon-long session often provides interesting insights into each other's work and more often than not an agreeable degree of unanimity over the way things are headed. Often trends in bond markets will confirm what is happening in shares, and so on.

On the hour-long train journey Peter has got tired of rehearsing his script for the client meeting and concentrates instead on another task. Recently the firm decided to make a short video about technical analysis, how it works and the services it can offer. The video is to be targeted at potential new clients and will use the services of a well-known TV presenter, a friend of one of Peter's colleagues. Peter's job has been to rough out an outline of the voice-over for the video - ideal work for a boring train journey.

3.45pm

Mid-afternoon, and Peter is in the City heading for the client's office in a high-rise office block near the river. The meeting is uneventful, except for the fact that his ideas provoke a furious argument between several members of the client's staff. "Often our role is to pull out the pin, lob the grenade into the meeting, and then sit back and watch the fireworks", says Peter, drawing evident satisfaction from the fact that he is not the target of all the flak. "Our clients value the independent perspective we bring."

5.45pm

Peter leaves the clients arguing among each other, excuses himself and gets a taxi to his next meeting. This is an after-work gathering of the Society of

Technical Analysts, a body that has grown up over the years to promote education in and the development of the techniques of technical analysis. The meetings take place monthly and Peter normally attends if he can, although his active involvement in the Society's affairs ceased some years ago due to pressure of work. The members are mainly City professionals and people from a variety of financial markets, together with a few private individuals, often managing their own money.

The speaker is an American computer boffin, explaining some abstruse theory which Peter finds rather too esoteric for his no-nonsense approach to how charts and markets work, but he listens for a while and then slips away to catch his train home.

On the journey back, after perusing the market comment in the evening paper, he takes the opportunity to look through some training materials one of his colleagues has prepared. One of the major banks wants to train some of its overseas securities staff in the arcane mysteries of the futures and options market. Peter's colleague specialises in the area and has been asked to give the course. Peter's expert eye is needed just to make sure that the course material has been pitched at the right level for the intended recipients. A quick read through and he can see it has.

8.30pm

Driving home from the station, the car radio is tuned to the local news station, in case some major event has occurred which might have an impact on the markets. The news is all about the likelihood of a close vote on a particularly controversial piece of legislation going through parliament. Peter smiles to himself at the thought that politicians might feel they are controlling events, but that markets have already priced the appropriate degree of caution into many shares already and are discounting the likely result.

Back at home after a bite to eat and some time with his family, Peter switches on the TV and flicks to the teletext City pages, checking on the day's changes and making some notes of particularly large moves. Tomorrow morning he will inspect these particular charts to see if they look interesting.

9.45pm

Halfway through this process, one of the firm's US clients calls to ask his view on whether the chart of a particular company might indicate that a bid is in the offing. Peter promises to check the chart first thing in the morning and to fax a reply to the client before Wall Street's opening.

Weekends are a little less hectic but Peter takes time out on Sunday morning before taking his two sons off to a school football match, to check out the views of the market pundits in the Sunday papers' business sections, and to look at the share tips, making a mental note to pull out the charts of two or three of them once back in the office the following morning.

If all this gives the impression that Peter is a bit of a market junkie, he is. Most people who work in his firm are too. "I've always been fascinated by the way markets work", he confesses. "In this job, it does help. But what it means is that you're very rarely off duty. Even when I'm on holiday I nearly always try to hunt down a copy of the FT every day."

TEN

THE CHARTING QUIZ

Having ground your way through the book to this page, it matters to me that I have written it so you can understand the contents. As a bit of fun I have set some questions which will test your memory retention. Try them. And if you have to, don't feel guilty that you need to go back and check on things. I would be surprised if you don't need to do so and to some extent I hope that you will. It's part of the revision process.

The questions come in three levels of difficulty, or obscurity, depending on what you have understood. Take your time - there's no limit on how long you take. Consider your answers carefully and keep your score on each section. You should score at least 7/10 before you move on to the next level. **The answers are given on page 128 onwards.**

LEVEL ONE

Q1   What are the two kinds of grid used by chartists called?

Q2   How many points of contact are needed for a trendline to be considered valid?

Q3   Name the three common continuation patterns.

Q4   What is the normal maximum number of weeks that a 'flag' pattern should take to build?

Q5   In the classic reversal patterns, the Double Top and Head and Shoulders, what should you always wait for before acting upon them?

Q6   How do you calculate Relative Strength?

Q7   On the ROC Indicator, what are the normal overbought and oversold levels?

Q8   The Golden Cross and Dead Cross moving average patterns are only valid if what criterion is in place?

Q9   Where in a stockmarket cycle would you expect to see very high levels of business done?

Q10   How can you undertake further reading without incurring huge costs, while at the same time enjoying other privileges?

LEVEL TWO

The charts in this section are taken from my company's Monthly Chart Book publication. I have used these specifically because of their timescales. They are typical of the kind of charts used by City analysts and contain the sort of detail for you to make sure you have got to grips with the techniques described in this book.

In the book I have used many stylized illustrations for the sake of simplicity and ease of understanding for the novice. This series of Questions and Answers is intended to develop your pattern recognition skills in the real world. The charts are mostly on logarithmic scales and the UK companies are daily bars; Continental stocks are plotted on a daily close basis. The moving averages, represented by dashed lines, are 200 days and the relative strength curve is a weekly calculation against the FT-Actuaries All Share Index, in the case of the UK stocks, and against the local market index for overseas stocks. The inset 9 year charts are monthly high/low plots which set the 4 year history into perspective.

Q1   Identify the primary trendline in the Dow Jones Home Bonds Index. Please note that this is an arithmetically scaled chart.

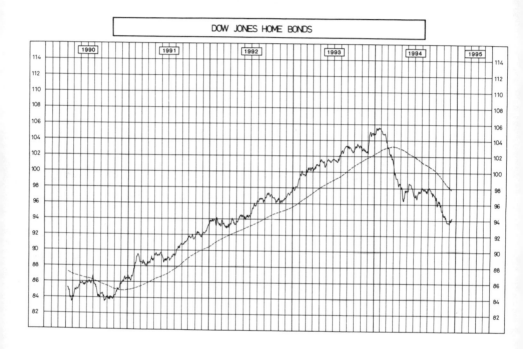

DOW JONES HOME BONDS

Q2 Can you identify the two distinct 'flag' patterns which developed during the sharp fall in Clyde Petroleum's share price in 1992? Please ring them with a pencil circle.

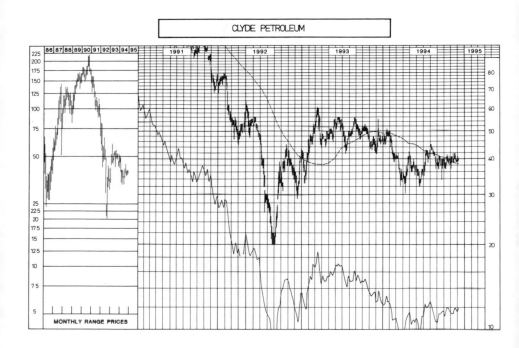

Q3 Identify the rectangle in the chart of Carlton Communications which heralded a rise of over 25%.

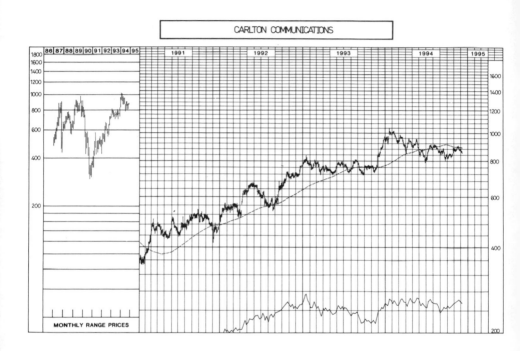

Q4 Using the measuring technique, can you calculate the target price following the completion of the "double bottom" pattern in BPB Industries in 1992/93.

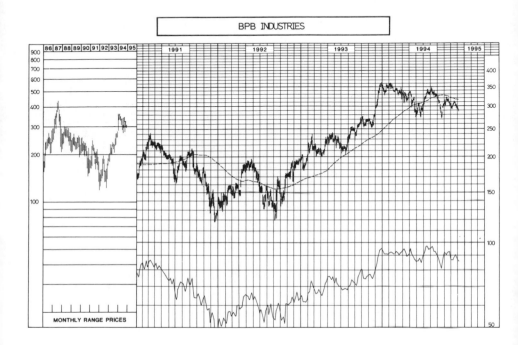

BPB INDUSTRIES

MONTHLY RANGE PRICES

Q5   The chart of Abbey National shows a clear support level which has not yet been broken. At what level is this support and where would you put in a stop-loss? This question will also give you practice at reading scales.

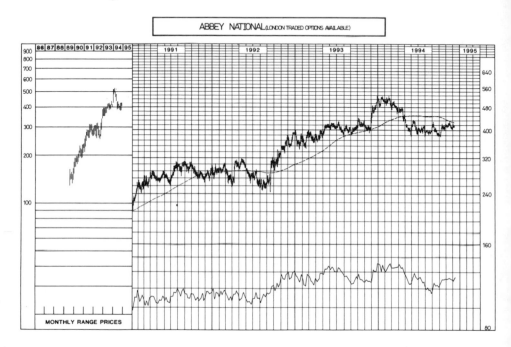

Q6 Identify and draw in the 'triangle' pattern in Eurodisney in 1994 and calculate the target price upon its completion. This chart is plotted on a daily close basis.

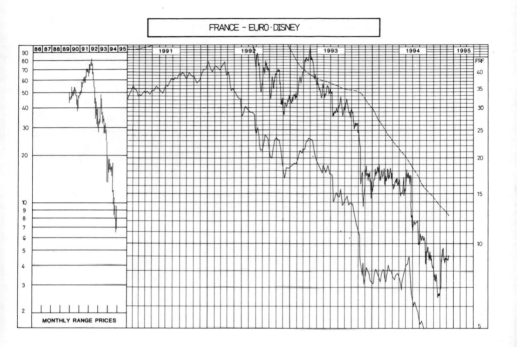

FRANCE – EURO·DISNEY

MONTHLY RANGE PRICES

Q7   The chart of Electrolux currently shows a well-defined support
level. At what price would you put in your stop-loss to sell? This
chart is plotted on a daily close basis.

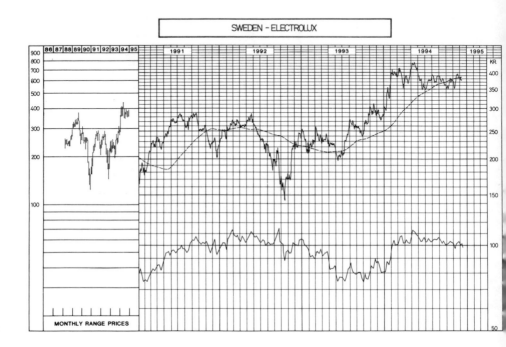

Q8 Find the important 'flag' and 'triangle' patterns which developed in Tadpole Technology. Mark them on the chart in pencil.

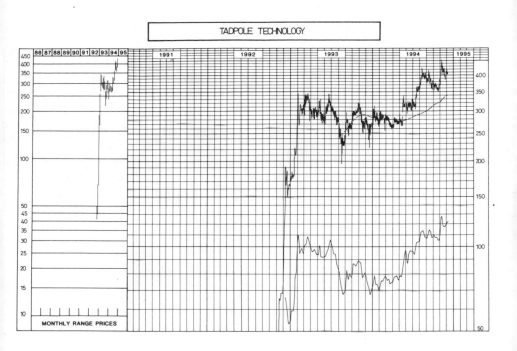

TADPOLE TECHNOLOGY

MONTHLY RANGE PRICES

Q9   The chart of Whessoe shows a clear 'double top' which built up during 1992/94. Draw in the neckline and calculate the downward prediction for the subsequent fall in the price.

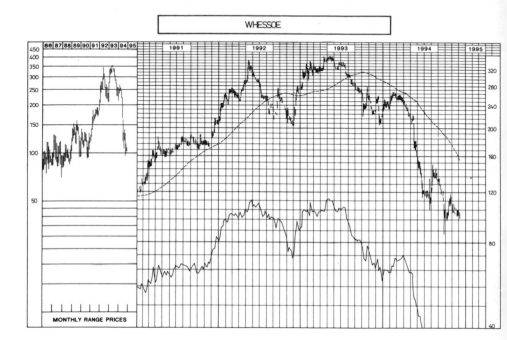

Q10 Stakis shows a 'double bottom' in 1992 and a series of 'flags' and 'triangles' on the way up. Draw in the rectangle which is currently building. At what level would you buy? At what level would you abandon your position in the shares?

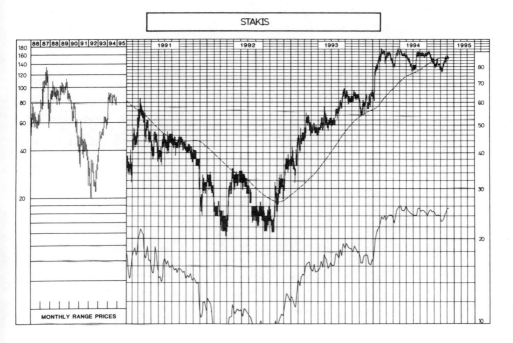

LEVEL THREE

We now move on. This set of questions will test your skills further. They are of a more advanced nature and I would be surprised if the newcomer will be able to answer them all without having to backtrack through the book for reference.

Q1   The chart of the Dow Jones Industrial Average is plotted on a daily high/low/close basis. The 20 day and 50 day moving averages cross each other on many occasions but only two of these crossovers are of interest to the chartist. See if you can identify them and remember their names.

Q2   On the same chart find the volume spikes which occurred in 1994. Why are they important?

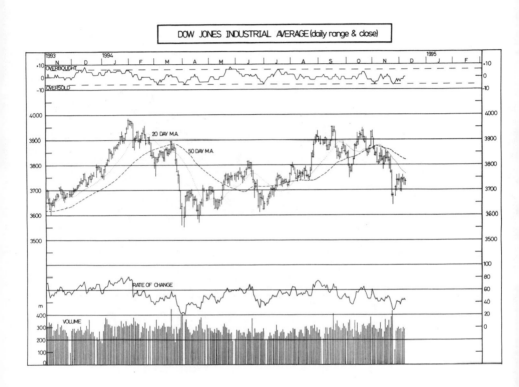

Q3   Find the important divergence between price and relative strength
on the chart of Kwik-Fit in 1993/94. Why was it important?

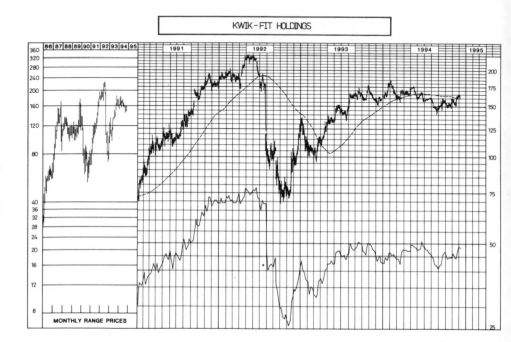

Q4 The clear top area in the price of NFC took almost two years to develop. How could you have avoided waiting in a dull share until the downward break in price finally came about?

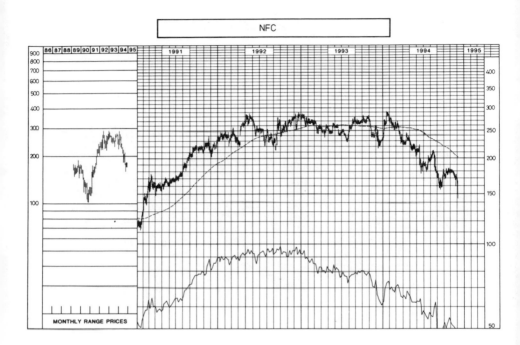

NFC

MONTHLY RANGE PRICES

Q5 The chart of HSBC shows a distinct 'Head and Shoulders' pattern building up. What should you do about it and when and at what price?

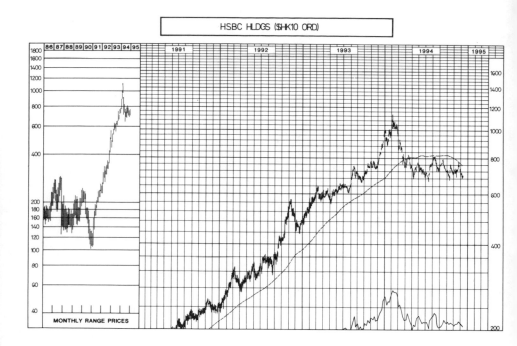

HSBC HLDGS ($HK10 ORD)

Q6   At the end of 1993 the shares of L'Oreal broke upwards from a 'triangle' at 1200 French francs. The move subsequently failed. Were there any indications on the chart as to why this might happen? Could the situation have been avoided?

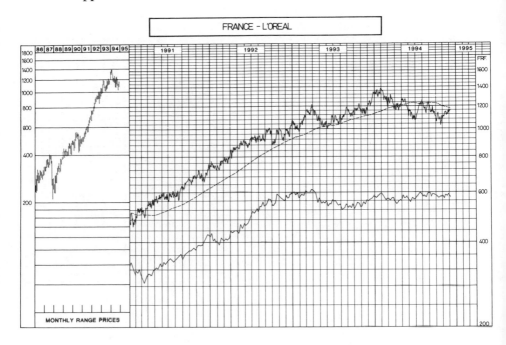

FRANCE - L'OREAL

MONTHLY RANGE PRICES

Q7 The chart of Reckitt and Colman shows a clear support level at 520p. But you should have sold long ago. Why?

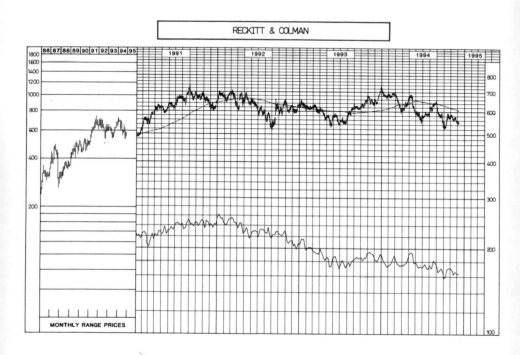

Q8   Chrysalis is a textbook chart (it's in this one!). See how many classic chart patterns you can find.

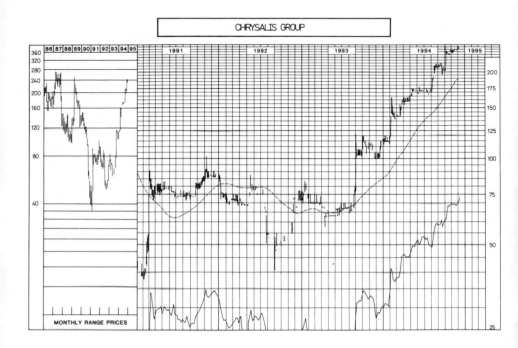

Q9 Staveley Industries has broken downwards through support at 195p but the price pattern suggests that further support could be present at 160p. What should you do if you are holding the shares?

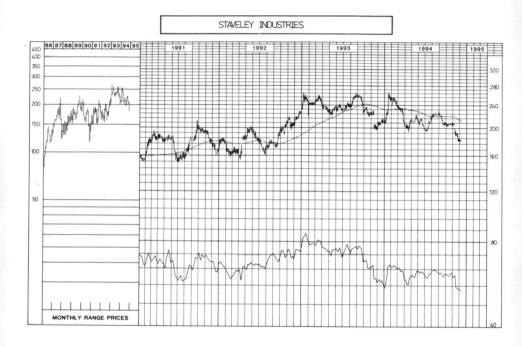

Q10 The chart of Vodafone shows a worrying development for the short-term trader although its long-term prospects look splendid. Why do I say this?

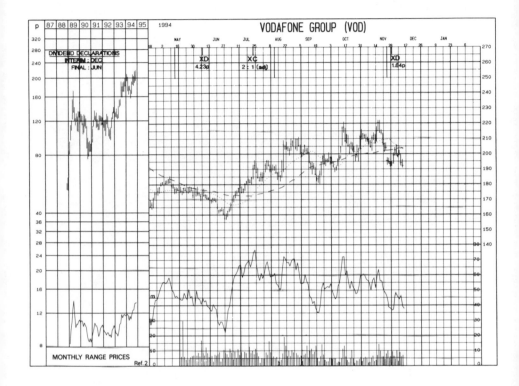

ANSWERS

LEVEL ONE ·

A1   Arithmetic and logarithmic

A2   Three

A3   Triangles, Rectangles and Flags

A4   Four

A5   Wait for the neckline to be broken

A6   Divide the share price by a market index

A7   70 and 30

A8   If both moving averages are moving in the same direction as each other

A9   At tops and bottoms

A10   Join The Society of Technical Analysts as an Associate Member

LEVEL TWO

A1   The uptrend is drawn on the chart. Its ending heralded a steep fall in bond prices in New York in 1994.

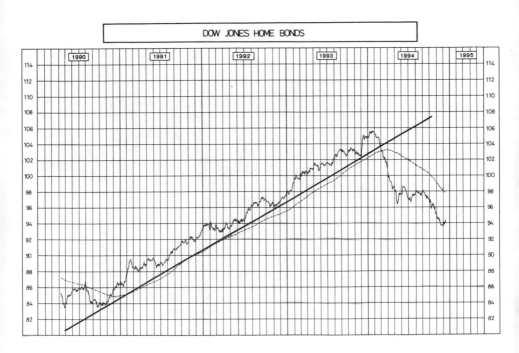

DOW JONES HOME BONDS

A2 Remember that flag patterns develop within a sharp move and usually last for no more than four weeks. Neither of these lasted longer than a fortnight but their effect on the share price was devastating.

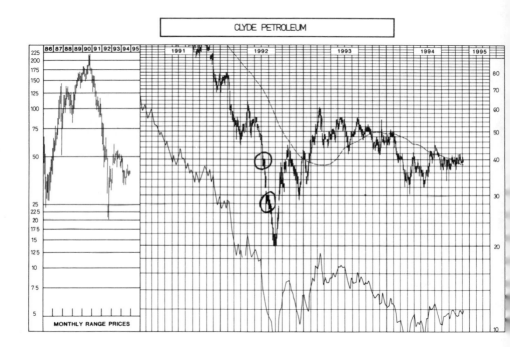

CLYDE PETROLEUM

MONTHLY RANGE PRICES

A3 The rectangle is a powerful chart pattern when completed. The upward break through 800p was a signal that the consolidation phase was over and the sprint to over 1000p in just over one month made profits for shareholders in very quick time.

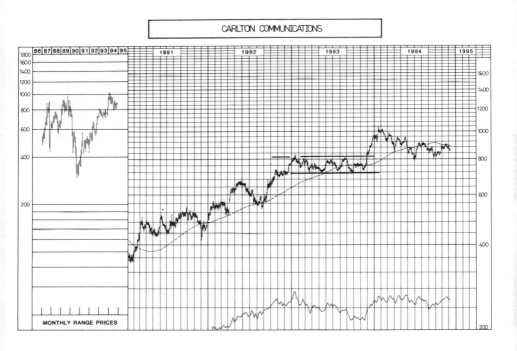

CARLTON COMMUNICATIONS

MONTHLY RANGE PRICES

A4   325p. The target is calculated by measuring the distance between the bottom and the neckline. For accuracy in making these measurements, a pair of dividers from the local stationers would be a good investment.

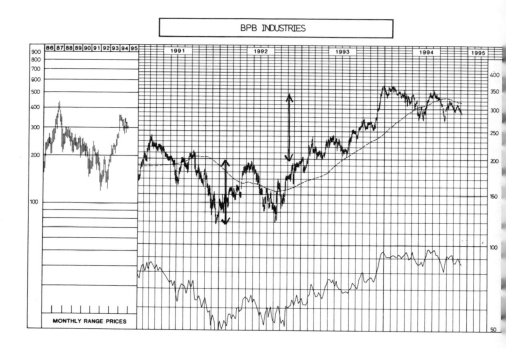

A5   380p. The scale is 16p per square so that the support is at 386p but allow for a margin in order to avoid false breakouts. 380p should suffice.

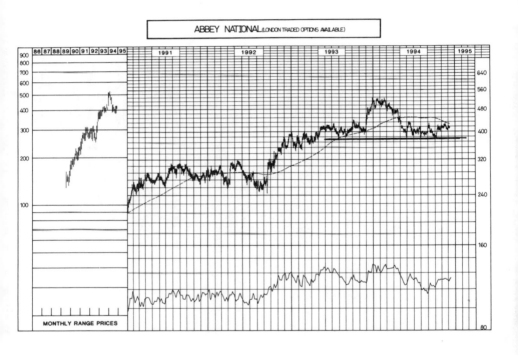

A6   The target is 11 Francs. This is calculated by taking the depth of the
triangle at its beginning and projecting the measurement down from
the point where the price breaks out of the triangle.

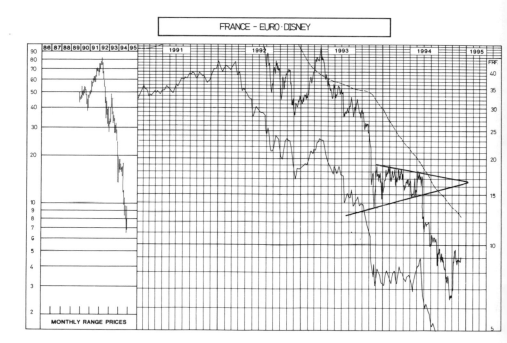

FRANCE – EURO·DISNEY

A7   Kr. 345. The support level is at 350. Leave a small margin of error.

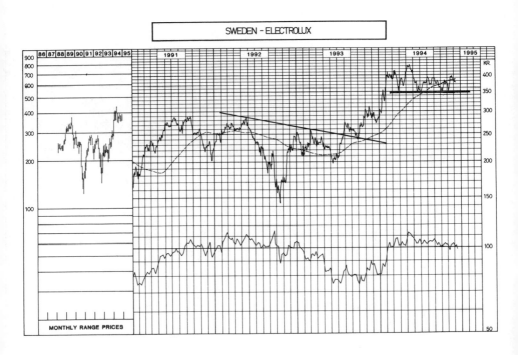

SWEDEN - ELECTROLUX

MONTHLY RANGE PRICES

A8   The flag and the triangle are marked on the chart.

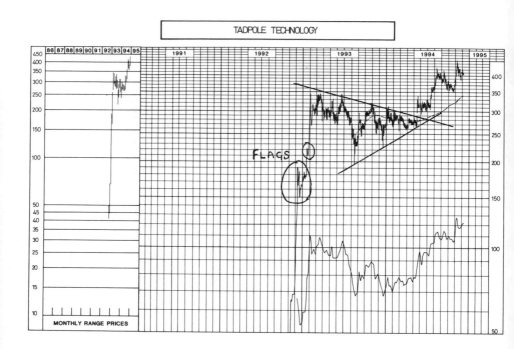

A9   120p. The formula for the calculation is to take the distance between the top and the neckline and project the result downwards from the point of the break.

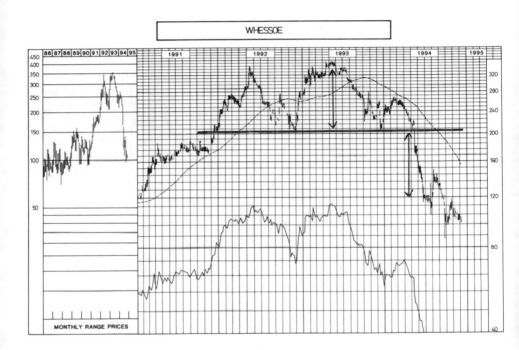

WHESSOE

MONTHLY RANGE PRICES

A10   The buying level is 95p, after leaving a small margin for error. A stop-loss at 76p would be the trigger point if instead the pattern broke downwards, or if things went wrong after a purchase on the upward break.

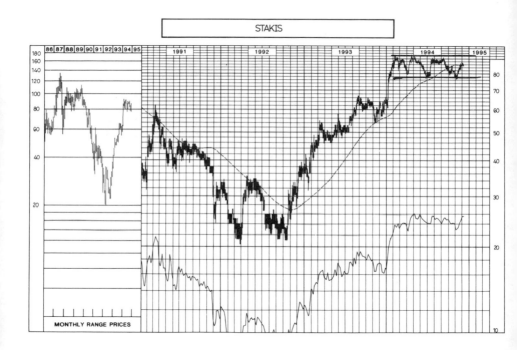

LEVEL THREE

A1 The Golden Cross and Dead Cross are marked on the chart for you. Remember that crossovers in the moving averages are only interesting if both of them are moving in the same direction.

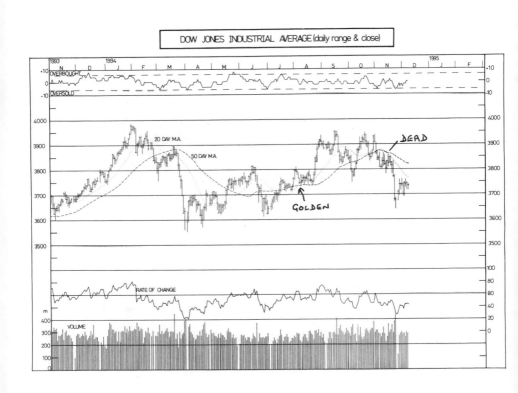

DOW JONES INDUSTRIAL AVERAGE (daily range & close)

A2   I have marked the volume spikes. They all occurred when the market was about to change direction. Only the really big spikes which occur much more infrequently are of interest to investors but short-term traders need to be nimble and these smaller volume spikes, although not always obvious at the time, can help as an early warning system.

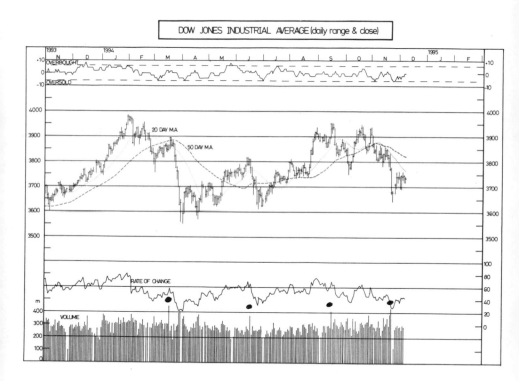

DOW JONES INDUSTRIAL AVERAGE (daily range & close)

A3   I have marked the divergence on the chart. The breaks into new high ground by the price were not confirmed by the relative strength and were therefore unreliable. Always look for confirmation as sometimes the strength of the overall market can pull up the price of an indifferent share.

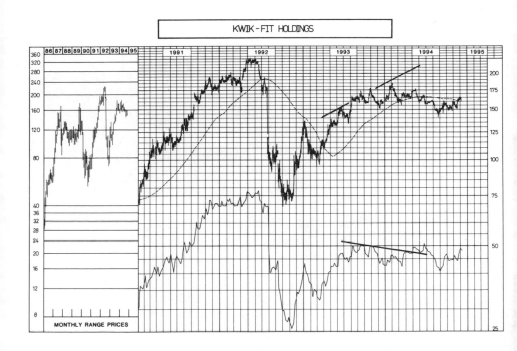

A4   The divergence is marked on the chart for you. Upward breaks in the share price which are not matched by confirmatory moves in relative strength can be dangerous and are best left alone. Although NFC was finding buyers at between 215p and 230p, the relative strength curve deteriorated throughout 1993 and was a clear warning that something was going wrong. The shares continued to lose ground against the FT-Actuaries All-Share Index throughout 1994.

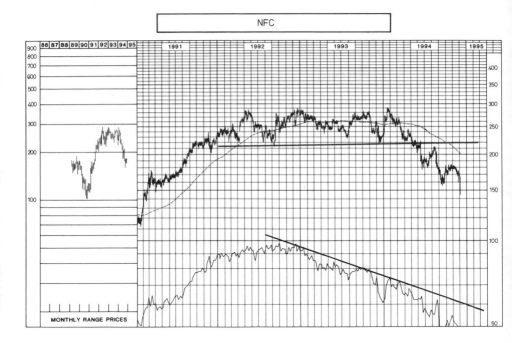

A5   The neckline has been drawn in for you and it will be seen that it has a slight left-to-right tilt. If anything, this makes it more potentially bearish. But with these patterns you must wait for the neckline to be broken. Potential head and shoulders patterns build up constantly in markets and shares but many are never confirmed.

Of course there will be occasions when you could sell as soon as you became aware of the threat and you curse later that you could have got out at a better price. But believe me, there will be many more of these patterns which never break the neckline and are therefore never validated. Patience is usually a virtue.

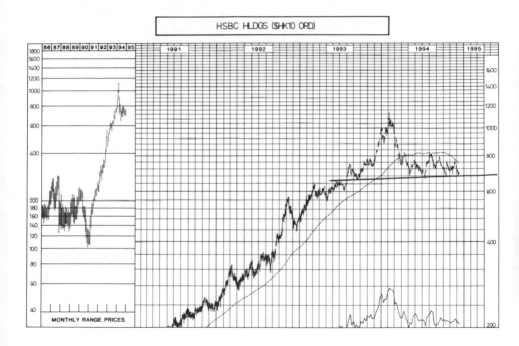

HSBC HLDGS ($HK10 ORD)

A6   The break was not confirmed by the relative strength curve. The price went into new high ground but the relative strength did not. I doubt that the situation would have been avoided in real life; I would have been tempted to buy but I would have been aware that this was not a perfect situation and that the dangers of a setback were, perhaps, above average.

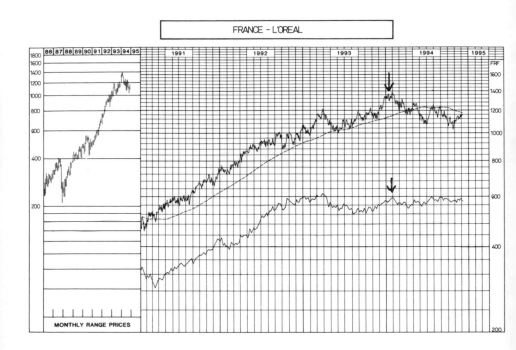

FRANCE - L'OREAL

MONTHLY RANGE PRICES

A7   Although support was present between 520p and 540p, the relative strength curve fell throughout 1992, 1993 and 1994. This was a warning that the support was getting a bit thin.

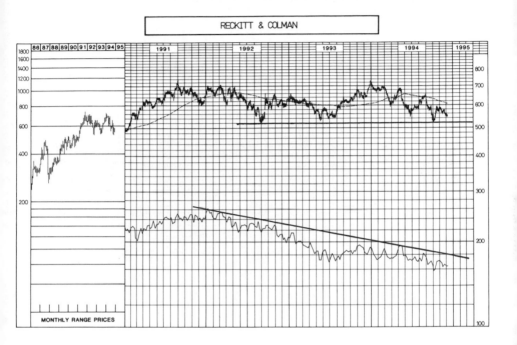

RECKITT & COLMAN

MONTHLY RANGE PRICES

145

A8   I have marked a Reverse Head and Shoulders neckline, a rectangle
and various flags. There is constant confirmation by the relative
strength that this is an above average share and the 200 day moving
average has been consistently saying that this is a bull market.

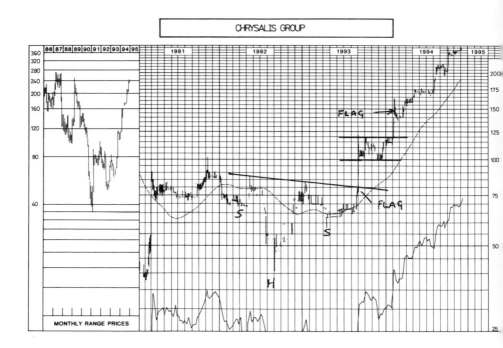

A9   When the support at 160p was laid down in 1991/92 the relative strength was comfortably above the 60 level. As the support at 200p has built during 1993/94 the relative strength has been below 60 on occasions. This suggests that the floor is weakening and that the potential support at 160p might not be as strong as the price chart alone would suggest.

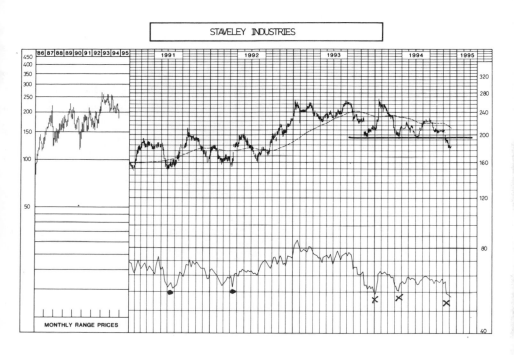

STAVELEY INDUSTRIES

MONTHLY RANGE PRICES

A10   Firstly, the uptrend from June/July has been broken. But more importantly there have been three moves into new high ground by the share price which have not been confirmed by the ROC indicator. This shows a very considerable divergence which I have marked on the chart. I am personally more impressed with the broken uptrend than the divergence for the reasons stated in the section on the ROC indicator but the weight of evidence builds up in the mind and such matters cannot be ignored completely.

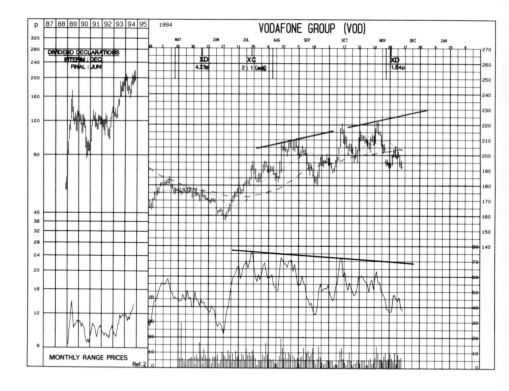

In this section you should aim for a score of at least 6/10 at your first attempt. Don't despair if you don't succeed first time. There is a lot to think about and a re-read of certain sections of the main book should soon put you right.

The whole point is to improve your familiarity with patterns and build up your interpretative skills. Spend as much time as you can in looking at all sorts of charts and make notes about your decisions and your reasons for them. You can then backtrack and see how your success rate improves.

APPENDIX ONE

FURTHER READING

Gifford, E., *The Investor's Guide to Technical Analysis,*
London, FT/Pitman Publishing, 1995

Murphy, J.J., *Technical Analysis of the Futures Markets,*
New York, New York Institute of Finance, 1986

Nison, S., *Japanese Candlestick Charting Techniques,*
New York, New York Institute of Finance, 1991

Pring, M.J., *Technical Analysis Explained,*
New York, McGraw - Hill, 2nd edn. 1985

Stewart, T.H., *How Charts Can Make You Money,*
London, Simon & Schuster, 1989

APPENDIX TWO

RATE OF CHANGE (R.O.C.) CALCULATION

(1) Date	(2) Close	(3) Up	(4) Down	(5) Up avg	(6) Down avg	(7) (5)÷(6)	(8) 1+(7)	(9) 100÷(8)	(10) 100-(9)
1	54.80								
2	56.80	2.00							
3	57.85	1.05							
4	59.85	2.00							
5	60.57	0.72							
6	61.10	0.53							
7	62.17	1.07							
8	60.60		1.57						
9	62.35	1.75							
10	62.15		0.20						
11	62.35	0.20							
12	61.45		0.90						
13	62.80	1.35							
14	61.37		1.43						
15	62.50	1.13/11.80	/4.10	.84	.29	2.90	3.90	25.64	74.36
16	62.57	0.07		.79	.27	2.93	3.93	25.45	74.55
17	60.80		1.77	.73	.38	1.92	2.92	34.25	65.75
18	59.37		1.43	.68	.46	1.48	2.48	40.32	59.68
19	60.35	0.98		.70	.43	1.63	2.63	38.02	61.98
20	62.35	2.00		.79	.40	1.98	2.98	33.56	66.44
21	62.17		0.18	.73	.38	1.92	2.92	34.25	65.75
22	62.55	0.38		.71	.35	2.03	3.03	33.00	67.00
23	64.55	2.00		.80	.32	2.50	3.50	28.57	71.43
24	64.37		0.18	.74	.31	2.39	3.39	29.50	70.50
25	65.30	0.93		.75	.29	2.59	3.59	27.86	72.14
26	64.42		0.88	.70	.33	2.12	3.12	32.05	67.95
27	62.90		1.52	.65	.42	1.55	2.55	39.22	60.78
28	61.60		1.30	.60	.48	1.25	2.25	44.44	55.56
29	62.05	0.45		.59	.45	1.31	2.31	43.29	56.71
30	60.05		2.00	.55	.56	0.98	1.98	50.51	49.49
31	59.70		0.35	.51	.55	0.93	1.93	51.81	48.19
32	60.90	1.20		.56	.51	1.10	2.10	47.62	52.38
33	60.25		0.65	.52	.52	1.00	2.00	50.00	50.00
34	58.27		1.98	.48	.62	0.77	.1.77	56.50	43.50
35	58.70	0.43		.48	.58	0.83	1.83	54.64	45.36
36	57.72		0.98	.45	.61	0.74	1.74	57.47	42.53
37	58.10	0.38		.45	.57	0.79	1.79	55.87	44.13
38	58.20	0.10		.43	.53	0.81	1.81	55.25	44.75

COLUMN 1:	Date
COLUMN 2:	Closing price for the day
COLUMN 3:	Amount the price closed UP from the previous day. (For example, on day 2, the price closed up 2.00 from day 1. Entry is made in Column 3 only if the price closed up from the previous day.)
COLUMN 4:	Amount the price closed DOWN from the previous day. (For example, on day 8, the price closed DOWN 1.57 from the close on day 7. Entry is made in Column 4 only if the price closed down from the previous day.)
COLUMN 5:	Value of the average UP close. (On day 15, you have the necessary information to begin calculating the ROC. Add all the values in Column 3 and obtain a sum of 11.80. Divide this sum by 14 to obtain the average UP close for the 14-day period. This value of .84 is put in Column 5. On subsequent days, you multiply the UP average by 13, add in any figure that might appear in Column 3 that day and divide by 14.)
COLUMN 6:	Value of the average DOWN close. (Add the down closes in Column 4 - a sum of 4.10. Divide this figure by 14 for the average down close and put this value of .29 in Column 6. On subsequent days, you multiply the last figure for the DOWN average by 13, add in any figure which appears in Column 4 and divide by 14. If no figure appears in Column 4, you just multiply by 13 and divide by 14.)
COLUMN 7:	Result of dividing the number in Column5 by the number in Column 6 (.84 ÷ .29 = 2.90).
COLUMN 8:	Result of adding 1.00 to the number in Column 7 (2.90 + 1.00 = 3.90).
COLUMN 9:	Result of dividing 100 by the number in Column 8 (100 ÷ 3,90 = 25.64).
COLUMN 10:	Value of the ROC indicator derived by subtracting the number in Column 9 from 100 (100 - 25.64 = 74.36).

INDEX

How To Make A Killing
in the
Alternative Investment Market

by
Michael Walters

*"Because I have limited capital, I often play in high risk,
high return situations."*
Michael Walters

This book can make you serious money. The Alternative Investment Market
(AIM) is one of the most exciting stockmarket opportunities for many years.
It allows you the chance to put your savings into the small and emerging
companies which will be forming this new market.

ISBN: 0-948035-14-5 **£9.95 Paperback**

Traded Options
– A Private Investor's Guide
How to invest more profitably
by
Peter Temple

"I believe that this book is a very useful addition to the increasing range of information on the subject, and will be of great use to those investors who are new to options as well as those who, having identified the potential benefits, require some guidance to enable their participation. At the same time, it is my sincere hope also that the book will go a long way to dispelling some of the myths that surround these products – myths which, like most others, are often based on hearsay rather than understanding, and which can tend, in effect, to prevent people making valuable discoveries for themselves."

David Hodson
Chief Executive, LIFFE

ISBN: 0-948035-06-4 **£16.95 Hardback**

The Second Financial Services Revolution

by
Brian Tora

"A prophetic glimpse of what is to come."
Financial Mail on Sunday
"Thought provoking . . . an authoritative commentary."
Money Marketing

An examination of the Retail Financial Services Industry and the wide ranging changes that seem inevitable as a consequence of regulatory and technological pressures. If you thought the first Financial Services Revolution – 'Big Bang' in the City and the introduction of the Financial Services Act – was traumatic, wait until you read about the second Financial Revolution which is taking place even now.

ISBN: 0-948035-10-2 **£12.95 Hardback**

The Private Investor's Guide to the Stockmarket

by
Neil Stapley

"Some say that money invested in the stockmarket should be money that the individual can afford to lose. THIS IS NONSENSE...
shares, like fine wines, sometimes take time to produce their best."
Neil Stapley

Written by one of the industry's leading practitioners, *The Private Investor's Guide to the Stockmarket* tells you how to increase your profits. It explains how the markets work and how to understand and trade in shares with the objective of building a portfolio which will provide both income and capital growth. There's advice on Personal Equity Plans (PEPs). For those willing to accept higher risks, financial derivatives (traded options that is!) offer the opportunity of greater rewards.

ISBN: 0-948035-11-0 **£8.95 Paperback**